seven
MORE DAYS

seven
MORE DAYS

Live a Life That's Bursting with
Positivity and Happiness …
Before It's Too Late

By Amy N. Dix

Published by Best Seller Publishing®, Pasadena, CA

Best Seller Publishing® is a registered trademark

Printed in the United States of America.

ISBN 978-1-946978-79-0

This publication is designed to provide accurate and authoritative information with regard to the subject matter covered. It is sold with the understanding that the publisher is not engaged in rendering legal, accounting, or other professional advice. If legal advice or other expert assistance is required, the services of a competent professional should be sought. The opinions expressed by the authors in this book are not endorsed by Best Seller Publishing® and are the sole responsibility of the author rendering the opinion.

Most Best Seller Publishing® titles are available at special quantity discounts for bulk purchases for sales promotions, premiums, fundraising, and educational use. Special versions or book excerpts can also be created to fit specific needs.

For more information, please write:

Best Seller Publishing®

1346 Walnut Street, #205

Pasadena, CA 91106

or call 1(626) 765 9750

Toll Free: 1(844) 850-3500

Visit us online at: www.BestSellerPublishing.org

Dedication

for "Lucy"

Table of Contents

A SPECIAL INVITATION FROM AMY

As I scroll through my Facebook memories every morning, I am reminded that I have been fighting for positivity for years. I see posts from more than ten years ago about living a positive, happy life—not just for my own benefit, but hoping to inspire others to do the same. So, although the story of this book may start at one point in my life, the fight has been happening for much longer. And I am not about to give up on that fight now. I realized that life is fleeting and the single most important thing in life is to be happy! My hope is that through this book and through the efforts of what we are doing in The Positive Life Company, we give you the tools, resources, and inspiration to not only be positive but also reach beyond to become bursting with happiness so that you can live the most fulfilled life and achieve anything you want to—before it's too late.

I would like to personally invite you to join The Positive Life Company communities. It's in these communities where we see lives transformed. These communities are about making a difference. They are about being a part of a movement.

Join our free community on Facebook at http://bit.ly/PLCComm. Whether you are just starting out in your positivity journey, or you've been at it for a while, you will find that you are right where you need to be in this community. We have many members who have been a part of The Positive Life Company movement since day one, and they will be there to support you, to love you, and ensure you do this crazy thing we call life in the best way possible!

Or, find a chapter in your area at http://thepositivelifeco.com/find-a-chapter/. If you don't see one in your area and are interested in starting a chapter for your community, please reach out.

Feel free to connect with me on any of the social networks. Send me or The Positive Life Company a direct message or comment anytime. I respond to all messages personally. Let's connect!

Foreword

By Jason Dix

I was somewhat nervous when my sister, Amy, asked me to write the foreword for this book, *Seven More Days*. All of my life, I have viewed my sister as an overachiever and somebody who was truly motivated in matters of business and professional success. These "views" are nothing short of reality. When we were in high school (I am two years older), Amy proved her ambition when she was selected to be the captain of the Lincoln Pius X High School tennis and dance teams. She took her talents with her to college at the University of Nebraska-Kearney and achieved the same honor, yet on a much more competitive and illustrious level. When 2003 came around, I had never been more proud of a human being than I was of my sister when she was selected to be the keynote speaker at the Honors Ceremony for her graduating class. She graduated in three and a half years and put my five-year extended-stay college plan to shame!

Perhaps it was during that honors speech, "Roots and Wings," that I realized the impact our parents had on our lives. As Amy talked to her fellow honors classmates, she encouraged them to remember the roots that were instilled within them during their college education so that they could grow their wings and soar in achieving anything that they wanted to achieve after graduation. Then she looked over at our parents and said, "I am grateful that my roots run deep not just in my college education, but in the lessons my parents raised me with. I am grateful that my wings are a result of my many life experiences during college, but they started to form well before now. It is through the encouragement and belief of my family that I have the honor to stand before you today."

Amy and I have definitely taken different paths in life, but through some sort of divine intervention, the Spirit of the Universe allowed us to both end up moving to Florida within a month of each other back in 2014. Seeing her grow as an author, entrepreneur, businesswoman, motivational speaker (the list goes on and on) has truly allowed me to see the fervor and talent she has in multiple areas of life.

From the day we received the phone call from my dad that our mom, Ronda, had been diagnosed with grade 4 brain cancer called glioblastoma, my sister was truly a cornerstone for the family. She created the website pinklipsticktherapy.com as a medium to communicate the positive aspects of my mom's life and her recovery. Through frequent collaboration with myself and my father, Amy constantly updated the world via the website and Facebook, allowing people to have comfort for the present and hope for the future.

While attempting to achieve the feeling of serenity, I recently went to play a round of golf with a friend who lives in North Beach Miami. He was struggling with his purpose in this life and was slowly realizing that his life experiences weren't necessarily outstanding whatsoever. He said, "I need to stop doing what I have been doing and start doing things that can transform my mind, because if I wrote my autobiography right now, that book would be boring!"

This made me think about how this book, **Seven More Days**, gives you, the reader, an opportunity to examine your life, learn about the history of psychological approaches as it relates to your personality archetype, take assessments that expose personal strengths and weaknesses, and stress the importance of the "interactions we all have with others and the impact those connections have on our ability to be happy," and all the while, engaging in activities that demonstrate the outcome of positive thinking on your overall happiness. The pages that lie ahead of you will allow you to realize that the summation of all our experiences in life are really outer expressions of inner thoughts. They will encourage you to think about your life (and death) in such a bold way that, even if by accident you picked up this book, it will be life transformational.

From one question Amy posed, "Mom, how can others live a life of positivity like you have?" she was led to not only research the effects of positivity on one's life but also dig deep into how our mom made it look so easy. You will learn the three components that my mom mastered when it came to positivity: Character, Connections, and Community. Grab a box of tissues as you near the end of this book and read Amy's letter to our mom, assuring her that the life lessons "Lucy" taught her will be demonstrated daily by her interactions with others. Amy also stresses that a life of "positivity, perseverance, and sheer happiness" is well within your capacity if you are committed to transforming your attitudes and lifestyles through various systematic processes.

If you are looking for inspiration, you have found it as it unfolds throughout this book. The depth of the subject matter will blow your mind. I encourage you to approach this with an open mind, a willingness to change your behavior, and honesty within yourself to examine your character defects, and to become committed to changing the negative thought patterns that you encounter.

The fact that you have picked up this book at all is proof that living positively and in the moment is a belief that is important to you. Amy will guide you through the super-simple steps on how to make a daily, conscious effort to shape your attitudes and emotions from negative to positive thinking. I hope you will embrace the journey you are on and remember that you truly are a beautiful human being. Through this book, you will not only strengthen your roots in positivity, but also receive from Amy your wings to happiness!

No Fear, No Regret

It may surprise you to know that the inspiration for a book about positivity came from the death of a loved one: my mother, Ronda Dix. Between April and December 2016, my mom was robbed of her vivacious life by an unexpected and cruel illness—a life event that hardly seems to lend itself to a book about the power of positivity!

But that heartbreaking experience got me thinking, and I finally concluded that, in fact, all life-coaching is simply death-coaching by a more positive name. Why? Because whenever we talk about living the best we can, we're really talking about making the most of the limited time we have on Earth and avoiding being consumed by regret when the end comes. A life coach may never refer to the Big D explicitly, but it is the ever-present elephant in the room.

My book is different: I want you to stop being paralyzed by the idea of death and start being galvanized by it.

To do that, we will first have to acknowledge that enormous elephant that takes up so much headspace. I believe it is only by looking Death squarely in the eye *now* and then, committing to living with true positivity that we'll be prepared one day to look at Death a final time and say what my mother said: "I am not afraid to die."

You'll get to know my mom, my muse, throughout the book, but now feels like a fitting time to introduce her to you.

Meet Ronda Dix

"I'll just be thankful if she makes it till Christmas," I recall saying to my cousin at the hospital. But it was only the beginning of April 2016, and we were still such a long way from my mother's favorite holiday.

Photo Credit: Abby Anderson, abbyanderson photography

Every year, the moment the Thanksgiving turkey had been digested, Ronda got giddy about decorating the house and the tree, and she reveled in gift-buying. Our Christmases were filled with love, laughter, and maybe a few libations. It would take us hours to open gifts; we would take the time to appreciate each one before opening the next, and my mom would be most excited about the gifts my brother and I got, even though she had been the one to buy and wrap them.

Of course, many of us love that time of year, too. There's the goodwill to all, the giving, the gathering, the singing, the warmth, and the sparkle—all uplifting things that bring the joy we need to sustain us through a long, gloomy winter. But Christmas was more than just an opportunity to eat, drink, and be merry for Ronda; for her, the holiday had extra positive associations because her mother had loved it, too.

Of all the wonderful Christmastime treats and traditions, the one I associate most with my mother is the tree. Her thing was ornaments. Wherever our family traveled, she would buy a souvenir ornament that she delighted in unwrapping when she decorated the tree. She took her time, reliving all her happiest memories one-by-one before hanging each of them on the tree. Her little baubles of bliss.

My mother was in a hospice facility by the time November finally rolled around, and I wondered how best to bring the holiday season to her. By harnessing the magic of social media, I was able reach out to friends and family across the world and ask everyone to send Ronda a tree ornament, one that somehow reminded them of her. The response was incredible: more than a hundred ornaments arrived.

Though my mom didn't live to see her final Christmas, her love of the holiday is part of the legacy she left to me, my brother, and my dad, and we will hang those gifted ornaments upon our Christmas tree every year to remind us of the many people whose lives Ronda touched during her sixty years on this planet.

In writing this book, my aim is to ensure that my mother can continue to touch lives. Through her well-lived life and her fearless death, she taught me so much about the power of positivity, and I want to now share those lessons with you.

I hope you'll continue reading and find out how you can ensure that, one day, you'll be able to look back on a life well-lived with no fear and no regret.

Are you ready? Then let's begin!

Part One:

A Framework for Positive Living

On a sunny day in November 2016, my dad called.

"This is it," he said. "You need to come home. We may have only seven more days."

This was the call I had been dreading since April 1, 2016—the day we found out that my mom had terminal brain cancer.

I raced to the airport nearest my home in Florida and boarded the plane to Nebraska, for what felt like my hundredth flight since April. I had been going home as often as I could to spend time with my mom and make whatever final memories there were left to be made. By this time, I was keeping a carry-on bag packed at all times, and I had left clothes at my parents' house so that, if necessary, I could go home for weeks without having to check a bag. On this flight, I was grateful for this strategy, knowing that every nanosecond waiting for the carousel to deliver my suitcase would have been torture.

The three-and-a-half-hour flight was torturous enough. There seemed to be less oxygen in the cabin than usual, and there was severe turbulence, although it was not the regular kind; the turbulence was inside of me. I was jolted by panic every time I thought that by the time I landed, I might have already lost my mother.

I leaned back against the headrest, and when I closed my eyes, I could see Mom perfectly, not as she had been since the illness took hold, but how I will always think of her. In this image, she is strikingly beautiful, with her piercing blue eyes framed by one of her many pairs of designer glasses (expensive ones that she could afford because she worked for an eyecare company). I see her short but wildly curly, thick bleach-blond hair that somehow looked different every single day because, rather than brushing and styling it, she would just tousle it with her fingers when she got out of the shower and wear her hair however it landed. And I see her hands clearly, with their long, slender fingers; hands that, unlike her smooth face, showed her age and the accumulation of life's worries. I knew she'd had plenty of worries and plenty of loss throughout her life, so how did she remain so upbeat?

After receiving the prognosis of certain death, Mom had told me, "I'm not afraid to die," and I had asked her how she could possibly not be scared. She replied, "Because I know that I will be in a better place and I have already lived such a wonderful life!" But during that fateful flight, I wondered if she would she still be upbeat now that death was no longer an abstract concept, and I made a vow to myself then that, if she had retained that optimism, I would get some answers from her.

*I was desperate to glean any last bits of advice from my mom before she took her last breath. After all, she had so much love and life, and so many lessons to share with the world. So, I took a list of questions with me folded in my pocket on my last flight home and hoped that I would have as many as **seven more days** to uncover the secrets of her positivity.*

In Part One, we'll lay the groundwork for parts two through four. We'll explore the nature and benefits of positivity in general, but more importantly, we'll delve more deeply into *your* life by finding out what's important to you so that you have a personal framework upon which to hang your newfound positivity. You'll do this by doing something brave: by putting yourself in Ronda Dix's shoes and imagining that you've come to the end of your innings. I understand this sounds scary, but don't worry; my mom always wore very comfy shoes, so they won't hurt you a bit—in fact you might decide to never take them off!

Chapter 1

Seven More Days

My mom never lived a life of extravagance or worldly travels. She never led any missions or did anything especially crazy. For all intents and purposes, she lived a pretty simple life—a life filled with friends, family, a normal job, long walks, and a lot of love. So, one might think that at the end of her life, she would have wished she had done more, explored more, or been more. Not Ronda. She was completely satisfied and thankful for what she achieved, the places she had been, the family she had raised: she attained her simple American Dream—one that so many middle-class Americans of her generation believed in.

But people like my mom are becoming the exception rather than the rule, and there is a profound need for my mom's message right now because a growing body of research is telling us that there's a serious happiness crisis in the United States as a whole.

How Happy Are You?

First published in 2012, the World Happiness Report (WHR)[1] ranks 155 countries according to their level of happiness, and

---

[1] http://worldhappiness.report/

the framework used by the researchers is interesting: they assess happiness using six "underlying variables":

+ Log GDP income per capita (a measure of income inequality)
+ Healthy life expectancy
+ Social support
+ Freedom to make life choices
+ Generosity of donations
+ Perceived corruption of government and businesses

The WHR released on World Happiness Day (March 20), 2017,[2] showed that in ten years the United States has fallen from 3rd to 19th in the happiness ranking of 34 countries in the OECD (Organization of Economic Cooperation Development). A remarkable drop—so remarkable, in fact, that the 2017 report dedicates an entire chapter to the happiness problem in the United States.

Chapter 7 of the 2017 WHR, entitled "Restoring American Happiness," shows that although the United States improved its happiness score in income and life expectancy (economic variables), the other four "social" scores plummeted. The result? As much proof as we're going to get that money cannot buy happiness (and that means getting that long-promised tax cut won't make much difference to your happiness bottom line). It seems the American Dream has turned into an American Nightmare.

---

[2] http://worldhappiness.report/ed/2017/

But don't we have more resources than ever? Aren't we better connected than we've ever been thanks to social media? Apparently, the Dream and the wealth don't matter to Americans anymore; we are being made too miserable by prevalent inequality, corruption, distrust, and social isolation to appreciate what we have. The author of chapter 7 of the report suggests there are five reasons for the US crisis of unhappiness:

- Big-bucks politics dominated by special interests
- Wealth inequity
- Rate of immigration and community segregation
- Repercussions of 9/11 attacks
- Declining education system

This is not a political book, so we won't be exploring these factors, but they're something to think about when you consider the broader socioeconomic context of your own happiness.

Activity: Personal Happiness Audit

For fun, let's adapt the six WHR criteria and use them to think about our own lives in those terms. In the table below, score yourself from -3 to +3 (0 = neutral).

VARIABLE	Example	My Score
My financial situation	+ 3	
My physical health	+ 2	
My mental health	+ 3	
My network of friends and family (exc. online networks)	- 1	
My freedom to make life choices	+ 1	
Donations I've given so far this year ($ and/or time)	- 1	
My trust in government agencies	0	
My trust in corporations	- 3	
Plus-Total minus Negative-Total *Maximum: +24* *Minimum: - 24*	+ 4	

How did you do? Hopefully, your score is in the plus range! Of course, this is just a snapshot using very broad criteria, but it can contribute to building a better understanding of your own happiness going forward.

The World Happiness Report gives us the big picture of our world, but it suggests that living in a deeply dissatisfied society is bound to have a negative effect on us as individuals. And we can see it with our own eyes. They're everywhere: those people who seem to hate the world, the people around them, and (worst of all) themselves. My speaking career has taken me various places in this world, and I am always embarrassed for people when I see how poorly they treat the customer service representative at the airport, the hotel clerk, or even passing strangers. It amazes me because it's far harder to be rude, grumpy, and disrespectful than it is to smile to the person on the other side of the desk and ask, "How is your day going?"

You catch more flies with honey, as they say, but it would appear that too many people did not get that memo. We've become a nation of complainers, a population that enjoys relaying the details of our encounter with the inept barista loudly into our cell phones to someone on the other end who probably had their own tale of woe to share. You only have to look at the drama-filled nightly news to know that we're addicted to the rage that perceived injustice and imbecility creates. In psychological terms, this tendency is called "negativity bias" and it serves a function in our survival; after all, it would be foolish not to take notice of a fire alarm! But things have gone too far. Everybody is responding to everything news media is telling us as a threat, and I don't know about you, but I'm exhausted by it!

We are so focused on ourselves and our own problems that we don't stop to think that others may just have it worse than we do. We've all been there. We forget that everyone deserves a pleasurable experience with us, even if it's just for a moment. How are we ever going to be happier and live a more authentic life if we can't even bestow a little happiness upon others?

Worryingly, the behaviors I've observed in daily life are backed up by Chapter 7 of the WHR, which states that research shows that between 2001 and 2011 there had been a serious decline in the "helping behavior" of Americans toward strangers (incidentally, this was not found to be true of our Canadian cousins).

I believe we project our perceptions of ourselves upon others. If we treat others like they are nothing, it's because we feel deep down that we are nothing; if we approach situations negatively, it's because we feel we have little to give; and if we put others down, it's because we lack self-confidence. If our actions mirror our internal thoughts, how can we change? Oftentimes, the advice given by "gurus" is that you need to change your actions in order to live a happier, more fulfilled life. I don't believe this at all. **I believe that when we change our thoughts, our actions follow**, a principle we will look at in more detail in later chapters.

The American chapter of the World Happiness Report ends with an appeal for US politicians to focus their efforts on rebuilding so-called social capital, which refers to the network of human relationships. But we cannot sit back and wait for the folks on Capitol Hill to improve our nation's happiness! Rather, we must do it for ourselves, and that begins with figuring out what is truly important to us as individuals.

> ** "Keep your face to the sun and you will never see the shadows. "**

—Helen Keller, American author and activist

Identifying Happy: The Seven Days Method

In the process of identifying what makes you happy, you're about to confront your worst fear.

Nobody is ever overjoyed by the prospect of their life's conclusion. Even those who choose to take their own lives—as too many in America today are doing—they do so with deep anguish. I doubt anybody has ever jumped off a bridge to certain death with a whoop of glee. So, how on Earth would thinking about your own death help you on the route to happiness?

You may have already wondered what you would do if you were to fall ill and be given a short time left to live. What great places might you explore? What things would you get to cross off your bucket list? What actions would you take? Maybe you would backpack through Europe. Maybe you would go skydiving, or even write your life story so that your children and descendants could know who you were and what you achieved.

But how would your answer change if you knew that you had only *seven more days* left to live? Oh, and by the way, you can't walk, feed yourself, or even get up to use the restroom. You just have to lie there and die. What would you do? Your answer changes drastically. In fact, the reality is that your answer is probably "nothing," you will do nothing. I don't mean to sound insulting, but I doubt you would be okay with the scenario. More likely, you would feel unfulfilled, angry, and scared. You're only human, after all!

This scenario lies at the heart of this book, so I want you to dedicate some real thought to it, as uncomfortable as that may feel, because when you have only *seven more days* left to live in a disabled state, you don't really get to choose what your next accomplishment will be. Instead, you need to know that your time on Earth was the best that it could be. This is why my mom's story—her satisfaction of life on her own deathbed—is so extraordinary and bold.

Activity: End-of-Life Meditation

Give yourself five minutes and find a quiet place to lie down. Make sure you aren't going to be interrupted.

Visualize a Christmas tree that has not been decorated, its branches completely bare. This tree represents the years you have lived so far, and you're going to decorate it with ornaments that represent your most notable achievements and your most treasured people or memories. These are the people, places, and situations that you feel good about.

Now, in your mind, pull out a box and open it up.

What is the first ornament you find? What form does it take? What or whom does it represent? Hold it, study it, appreciate it.

Because this is your first thought, it is probably the most important, so you should hang it high on the tree.

Keep pulling out ornaments, each symbolic of the things you feel good about, and imagine hanging them on the tree at various levels, depending on the position of importance of what they stand for in your life.

When you have finished, step back to admire your tree. Hopefully, you have plenty to feel good about!

But there is another box in your attic you haven't opened yet, a box full of broken ornaments. These represent the things in life you have not yet achieved, the relationships in your life you have neglected or spoiled, the places you didn't go.

Do not skip this part of the meditation, even though this box is more painful. By sorting through those broken ornaments, you can identify the ones you can fix. These represent promises to yourself: these ornaments WILL be added to your tree before you die.

Some ornaments, however, might be broken beyond repair. When you find one of these, hold it in your hand for a moment, thank it for being a lesson for you, and throw it into a garbage chute. Let it go.

Keep the fixable ornaments in the box for now but remember what is in there. As you apply the insights from your meditation in your life, you will begin to empty this box of its broken ornaments and add them to your tree of things you feel good about.

I believe that the best way to live your best life is to practice dying. Of course, I am not asking you to do something crazy like jump off a cliff to see if you will live or not! I simply want to prepare your mind for the moment of death and encourage you to truly consider, what business have you left unfinished? Whom have you hurt in your life that you may want to make amends with? What advice do you want to give your children that you never gave? What wisdom do you want to pass along to your grandchildren that you never had the opportunity to share?

It's common for people who know they are dying to feel hopeless, depressed, sad, or scared. If you were feeling those things, imagine now, how that might affect your loved ones. They likely would feel scared and hopeless too. There would be chaos around the time of your death because everyone would be scrambling to make the rest of your days *good* days.

But, what if you could feel fulfilled, at peace, and grateful. Now, imagine how your loved ones may take on a sense of relief that you know you've lived an incredible life and are at peace during your transitioning. Now, we create an environment of love, calm, and peace. This is possible when you choose a life of positivity, celebrations, and love. But, this is a CHOICE—it's an effort that you must make every day. We must all choose our life carefully because we don't get to choose our death. It was a choice my mom made, and by living a simple, positive, authentic life, she felt complete fulfillment—even on her deathbed.

And her secret? Ronda Dix mastered three things in life—character, connections, and community—that we will explore later in the book, so you too can live a more positive life and be completely fulfilled, even if you have only *seven more days* left to live.

“*I have come to know that it [death] is an important thing to keep in mind— not to complain or to make melancholy, but simply because only with the honest knowledge that one day I will die I can ever truly begin to live.* **”**

—R.A. Salvatore, The Halfling's Gem

Chapter 2

Defining Positivity

What is positivity?

It seems like an easy question on the face of it. Many of us would answer it by saying that positivity is simply looking on the bright side of life, right? It's looking for the good in everything and putting an upbeat spin on whatever may have gone wrong for you that day.

But think about it. Would you really want to spend much time with someone who went around smiling incessantly and declaring "Problem? What problem? Why, everything's just wonderful!" That person would soon find themselves in an empty room (although, annoyingly, he or she would probably think, *How nice! Quiet time*).

People who are relentlessly chipper are irritating, let's face it. But why? I suspect it's because we know they have bad days, just like we do. We think, *They can't possibly be that happy*, and so we see their positivity as a facade. At best, they are simply protecting us from the negative effects of their bad day; at worst, they are lying to us about their lives.

But always putting on a brave face is not the whole story of positivity, nowhere close. To get a grip on the complexity of what we mean by "positivity," we need to get granular and examine the parts that make up the whole. Only then can we recognize positivity in others and build those qualities we admire into our own behaviors.

Here are the characteristics of positivity as I see them (listed alphabetically, not in order of any importance). Not all positive people will have all these characteristics, and some characteristics will be stronger than others, but they will have a mix of them.

Acceptance

Not worrying or raging about what you cannot control or change.

Active

Physically active. Enjoying the outdoors and the movement of your body.

Conscientiousness

Enjoying the work and its challenges, whatever the job.

Curiosity

Closely observing life, love, and the universe—and being wowed by what you discover.

Gratitude

Thankful for the little things.

Humility

Recognizing that you don't know/can't do everything and handling valid criticism with grace. Belief in higher power.

Humor

Being able to laugh at the absurdity of life and at yourself.

Optimism

Expecting the best outcome of a situation. Seeing the best in a bad situation.

Presence

Enjoying the here and now.

Prospective

Hopeful for the future, not mired in retrospection.

Resilience

The ability to get back up again after you've been knocked down.

Self-esteem

Deep, unshakeable belief in your own value.

Take a moment to consider how each of these qualities fits into your personality right now. Perhaps place a tick next to the ones you feel you've got in your toolbox, a question mark next to those you're not sure you have in sufficient quantity, and a cross next to the qualities you know you do not currently have and need to work on.

If those are the characteristics of positivity, what are the benefits? In my opinion, these are just some of the benefits. What additional ones can you think of?

Benefits of Positivity

I believe the benefits of incorporating positivity in your life include:

1. Achieving goals and success in things you want out of life—dare I say, achieving anything you want
2. Succeeding easier and faster
3. More happiness in general
4. More energy
5. Greater inner power and strength
6. The ability to inspire and motivate others by example
7. Experiencing fewer difficulties along the way
8. The ability to surmount any difficulty

9. Seeing life smile back at you
10. Respect from others

I believe that, at its core, positivity is defined by choice. It is a personal decision we make 100 times a day. I believe we can identify when we are or are not being positive and change our behavior. Sometimes it is hard work in the moment, for sure, but for me it is a much less stressful, more authentic way of living in the long term.

> **"** *It will never rain roses: when we want to have more roses, we must plant more roses.* **"**
>
> **- George Eliot, English novelist**

So, we've looked at what positivity is, but what about what it isn't?

Positivity is not delusional: While we all connect well with upbeat people, positivity can be grating when someone has lost touch with reality (as we talked about at the start of this chapter). It's natural for people to want to believe in a good outcome, even when one is not possible. When my mom was in the hospital, it was tempting to say, "She's gonna live five more years! We're gonna beat this thing!" But that was not the reality, and I believe that optimism becomes denial in these sorts of situations, stopping people from dealing in the healthiest way with unpleasant truths.

This is how I like to explain it. If you're happily driving along the right-hand lane of the interstate and you come up behind a semi-truck that's going slowly, you have two choices. You can slow down and remain in that lane, accepting that you're not going to get to go where you need to go on time. Or, you can pass the semi and enter a faster lane, even if it's scarier than the right lane—the positivity lane. By overtaking the semi, you enter the reality lane, because sometimes you have to accept the reality and pass the obstacle before you can get back into the positivity lane.

Of course, I understand that everyone approaches these obstacles in different ways. People cope in different ways, at different times, at different speeds. We saw this with my brother, Jason. As my mom tried to have this "I am dying" conversation with my brother, he simply stopped her and said, "Mom, let's not talk about that. Let's talk about what we are going to do for your eightieth birthday!" (She was only fifty-nine years old.)

This is classic denial and escape behavior. This was his coping strategy. A coping strategy refers to "how people actually respond to stress as they contend with real-life problems."[3] He also was trying to only focus on being optimistic, which simply was not realistic. In positive psychology, we call this unrealistic optimism, "wishful thinking." While my brother was wishful thinking, my mom immediately shut down.

---

[3] Skinner, E. A., & Zimmer-Gembeck, M. J. (2007). "The development of coping," *Annual Review of Psychology*, pg. 124

I was standing on the other side of my mom's hospital bed watching this conversation unfold. It was heartbreaking. I felt as if I were just a ghost in the room, like I was not living in reality. I didn't know what to say. I didn't know how to act. I was stunned. I was sad for my mom. I was mad at my brother. After all, how could he be so naïve as to say something like this? So, I cried…silently. Frozen in that moment.

It wasn't until days later that I came to grips with, what I thought at the time, was an ignorant and insensitive comment. I realized that just because I may have accepted the situation quickly, passed into that reality lane already, that didn't mean that my brother had. That also didn't mean that he was wrong, or that he had any ill-intention. He eventually came around and we were all in the same place about the reality of the situation.

I believe it's important to remember that there is not necessarily a right or a wrong way to cope. Sometimes it can be frustrating when others do not cope with stress the same way you do, but understanding why they may be feeling the way that they do is the best thing you can do to support them – to get them into the reality lane so they can get back to the positivity lane.

Positivity is not always the right choice: As I mentioned in Chapter 1, there is the concept of negativity bias, which is our brain's way of protecting us from endangering ourselves. We are programmed to watch out for negative factors in our environment and take defensive measures. Take skepticism as an example. This often is characterized as a negative quality, but if we ignore our doubts and stay in the positive lane, that makes us gullible, and being gullible makes us vulnerable.

Researcher Joseph Forgas[4] goes even further in his assessment of the positive benefits of negative emotion. In his paper entitled "Don't Worry, Be Sad! On the Cognitive, Motivational, and Interpersonal Benefits of Negative Mood," Forgas says that being melancholy can help us remember things, be more motivated, avoid mistakes, and empathize with others better.

Positivity is not self-satisfaction: There is also evidence to show that being too positive leads to a kind of selfishness, an "I'm-all-right" attitude, which results in living in our own blissful bubble to the exclusion of others. Positivity is, therefore, not extreme self-satisfaction. Some level of unhappiness has its benefits, and if we're angered by something, we're more likely to be engaged in our democracy or bettering our personal circumstances.

Positivity is not perfection: I think even the most positive people struggle with it, perhaps daily, because I know I do—and I run a business called The Positive Life Company! I'm not positive a hundred percent of the time: that's called perfection, and as we know, there is no such thing as perfect. Kicking yourself for failing to be positive can set you off down a negativity spiral, so I don't recommend it! You have to cut yourself some slack and say, "You know, I could've handled that better. Next time, I will … "

Shoot for progress, not perfection, and you will always succeed in improving.

---

[4] DOI: https://doi.org/10.1073/pnas.1411678112

Positivity is not an end in itself: Positivity is a means to an end, and that end is happiness. But "happiness" is not a clear-cut concept because we all define it differently. We'll talk more about your personal goals in a later section, but I would like to share with you my idea of happiness, which may resonate with you: I believe that **happiness is inner peace.**

I know this isn't original—Buddha got there first—but let's think about it for a moment. Happiness and inner peace aren't mutually exclusive. One can have a miserable existence but still be at peace in their inner core. This peace is what gives people the strength to sustain their tough lives, but this does not create joy. I know from experience you can be suffering at the loss of a loved one, whether through death or a breakup, and still be at peace inside. Inner peace is long-lasting and enables us to accept the dreadful with fortitude; a sense of happiness is but fleeting and fragile.

If you are constantly searching for that place of happiness, you may never find it. But when you *create* happiness, you can achieve it.

The way you create happiness is recognize positive moments and stay in those moments, even if brief.

3:1 Positivity Ratio

Psychologist Barbara Fredrickson developed the "golden ratio" for positivity.[5] She believes that for human beings to thrive,

---

5 Barbara Frederickson Ph.D., *POSITIVITY: Top-Notch Research Reveals the 3-to-1 Ration That Will Change Your Life* (New York: Harmony,

they need to experience three positive emotions to every one negative emotion. Fredrickson arrived at this theory because of an experiment involving students, which showed that a positivity ratio above 3 led to higher mental and social health.

When this notion was put forward in 2013, Fredrickson believed less than 20 percent of Americans were thriving, and it seems unlikely that the percentage will have changed much. It's my aim that you become one of the fortunate 20 percent.

Positivity and Science

So why is positivity so darn hard? It is due to the way our brain processes information. It is called *negativity bias*. The bias increases the negative and decreases the positive. Dr. Rick Hanson says it best in his book, *Hardwiring Happiness*, "Your brain is like Velcro for negative experiences but Teflon for positive ones."[6]

This is why the news reports negative stories—journalists know that humans are naturally attracted to negativity and drama. I stopped watching the news eight years ago and have never looked back. It's just too negative for me. If you think you must watch the news to stay informed, I promise you that if there is something urgent that you must know, you will find out in this interconnected world. Try it.

2009)

[6] Rick Hanson, Ph.D., *Hardwiring Happiness: The New Brain Science of Contentment, Calm, and Confidence,* (New York: Penguin Random House, 2013)

Speaking of drama, ever met that one person who, no matter what, has a negative comment for everything? Now, you know why—the negativity bias! They are in, what I call, the "spin cycle of negativity." They just keep spinning and can't get out!

So, you are fighting an uphill battle from the start! It's in our nature to hold on to negative experiences and push away positive ones. So, unless you make a conscious effort to "rewire" your brain, your life will be one of struggle, scandal, and strife.

Happiness lies within the prefrontal cortex (PFC) of our brains. In addition, neuroscientists have discovered that people who have a more cheerful disposition and are more prone to optimism have higher activity occurring in their left PFC. This supports a conclusion that positivity leads to happiness.

Dr. Jeffrey Schwartz, a leader in neuroplasticity (the brain's ability to change and adapt), suggests that you can change the makeup of your brain through self-directed neuroplasticity. This means that when you choose positivity over negativity, your brain starts to accept positivity as the norm. Thus, you can rewire your brain for positivity.[7]

In addition, science has shown a correlation between the brain, a person's positive attitude, and the body's response. Being positive can help an ailing body fight disease better and mentally take on the challenges. Even if you fail or don't get the results you want, it has been shown that it's easier to recover or continue in a positive frame of mind. For example, if you don't get a job you applied for, you don't want to fall apart. Instead,

---

[7] www.jeffreymschwartz.com (accessed December 2018)

you need to accept it and keep looking until you do eventually find one.

Therefore, the secret to happiness really is no secret at all. Our brain reveals the truth: positivity leads to happiness.

My mom understood this on a macro level. A macro level of life is your life as a whole—your entire life. It's how she got through the many challenges of her life. She understood that even though this one moment, this one incident, this one challenge was difficult, she didn't have to let it affect her entire life.

I have seen this time and time again in those who struggle with moments in their lives. They allow these moments to define them. They allow these moments to consume their actions and their choices. They allow these moments to provide them with excuses in life for the way they act and the way they choose to feel. This is when people give up on a macro level and allow these micro-moments to define their lives. You do not have to do that. Your unhappiness does not need to be defined by being abused as a child. Your unhappiness does not need to be defined by the fact that both of your brothers died too soon. Your unhappiness does not need to be defined by being burned as a young child. Your unhappiness does not need to be defined by being diagnosed with cancer. Your unhappiness does not need to be defined by watching your mom die. These are all things that happened to my mom, which she did not let define her overall life and happiness.

What micro-moments have you gone through that you are allowing to define your unhappiness? What micro-moments do you need to let go of? What micro-moments do you need to change your perspective of? On a micro level, this moment may be hard. It may be tough and feel impossible to get through. But on a macro level, your overall week, month, or life does not have to be defined by the micro level because your life can be (and will be) amazing when you choose overall positivity! Because when you choose positivity, you choose happiness!

> " *Even if happiness forgets about you a little bit, never completely forget about it.* "

—Jacques Prévert, French poet

Chapter 3

Building a Positive Outlook

As this book progresses, I'll be encouraging you to make some changes to your outlook to allow more positivity into your life. But I know that change can be hard, so I wanted to create some easy-to-remember tools to assist you. Changing your attitude and behaviors in the present isn't only about coping with day-to-day challenges; it is also about becoming a better version of yourself in the future, a version of yourself that has a protective shell of positivity, better able to weather life's disappointments and misfortunes.

Be in the Moment: Daily Practice

Life is a succession of moments. Short moments. Long moments. Negative moments. Positive moments. If we want to live a life that is bursting with positivity and happiness, it is our responsibility to create the most positive, impactful moments possible. This is the secret to happiness. Every moment is an opportunity: An opportunity to fail, an opportunity to succeed, an opportunity to remember or to forget. It is how we shape these opportunities that leads us to the best moments possible!

> *" The only time you ever have in which to learn anything or see anything or feel anything . . . or grow or heal is this moment, because this is the only moment any of us ever gets. You're only here now; you're only alive in this moment. "*

—Jon Kabat-Zinn, American educator

Every day we have a choice. We can set our day up for a streak of good moments, or we can leave it to chance. I don't know about you, but I want to set myself up for the opportunity to have the most amazing, happiest day of my life. I want an unbroken streak of the best moments possible for that day. It is a choice, and it's up to you to make the right choice.

To achieve this, I want you to follow the M.O.M.E.N.T. system. These life-transforming practices will lead you along the happiness trail so that you can achieve anything you want to in life. In just thirty minutes a day, you can elevate your entire day into the happiest day possible.

According to McKinsey Solutions, 70 percent of transformation programs fail.[8] In my opinion, there are two reasons for this: lack of momentum and lack of sustainability. Think about it, if you can't gain any momentum in your transformation, you will not see results, and quit. In addition, if you can't sustain the work you need to do to transform, you will quit by default.

It's just like training for a marathon. If you start out by running a half mile every day, but do not gain any momentum to improve and run further every day, you will never be able to complete the 26.2 miles. In the same sense, if you get the momentum and start running ten miles per day, but your body gives out and you can't sustain your long runs, you will never be able to run the entire 26.2 miles.

Once dedicated to the M.O.M.E.N.T. system, you must celebrate the momentum and sustain your efforts in order to achieve success! My recommendation would be to rise thirty minutes earlier every morning and make a commitment to start your day off on the best foot possible!

Before I reveal exactly how to implement this new practice in your daily life, I am going to say something that may shock you: according to a small study of twenty people I carried out for The Positive Life Company in March 2018, *70 percent of you reading this book will never implement these practices.* That's right, only 30 percent of you will actually commit to these practices.

---

[8] McKinsey & Company, "How Do I Implement Complex Change at Scale?" (2017), https://www.mckinsey.com/~/media/mckinsey/dotcom/client_service/public%20sector/pdfs/how_do_i_implement_complex_change_at_scale.ashx

If I could guarantee you more happiness in your life, wouldn't you jump on board? Truth is, most of you won't because it's a change and it takes work. Let's change these numbers! Now, I know 100 percent participation is not going to happen, but what if we were able to flip the statistic? What if 70 percent of the readers were to complete these daily practices? For example, if just 1,000 people read this book, that's 700 lives changed. That's 700 happier people in this world. We also know that these 700 people will not just be more positive and happy, they will also build their character, connections, and community, and in doing so, will impact others toward a better state of being. Even if these 700 people impact only 100 lives in one year (it will be more if they fully commit and do the practices everyday), that's 70,000 more lives impacted for the good in JUST ONE YEAR! We also know that because these 100 people were impacted by positivity and happiness, they will also have an effect on others, sort of a domino effect. Even if those 100 people in turn affect 5 people, that's 500 more people living a better life. Then these 500 will impact 5 more people, another 2,500 people, and on and on. Do you see the effect we can have when we all come together and make a commitment? In this example, we now have changed the lives of 73,800 people! You see, it's not just about YOU—it's truly about changing the WORLD!

So, what is the impact of a single person—YOU? When you commit to the M.O.M.E.N.T. daily practice, you can effectively change the happiness of over 3,000 people! Pretty incredible, right?

So, I urge you to not just read this next section, but to download the worksheet from our website (www.thepositivelifeco.com/seven-more-days) and start changing not just your life, but the world!

Through our study, 100 percent of those who committed to putting M.O.M.E.N.T. into practice increased their level of satisfaction in all areas: Positivity, Happiness, Character, Connections, Community, and "Achieve Anything" Goal.

After just seven days, the level of positivity increased by 12 percent, and the overall happiness satisfaction increased by 10 percent. So, start there; start with just seven days. Once you commit to the seven days, you will see how easy and effective it is. Then, commit to thirty days, and from there, it will just become a part of your life. Once it is integrated into your life, you are well on your way to transforming your life and others'. Imagine the life you will live. Imagine the goals you will CRUSH. Imagine the possibilities!

Now, let's get started! Just follow this mnemonic device, focusing on each practice for only five minutes.

- **M - Mute:** Be silent for five minutes with zero distractions.
- **O - Outcome:** Write down one outcome you must conquer today that will get you one step closer toward your "achieve anything" goal.
- **M - Memorize:** Identify and write down your daily phrase for today. Memorize it. Repeat it.
- **E - Express:** Express your feelings to a loved one.

- **N - Noble Act:** Identify an unselfish noble act you can do for someone today and implement it.
- **T - Terminate:** Terminate one thing in your life that is not bringing you positivity.

Let's look at these in more detail.

MUTE

"Silence is a source of great strength."

—Lao Tzu, Chinese Philosopher

In a digitally connected world, we now have more environmental stimuli than ever. Think about it: When was the last time you sat in complete silence with no distractions? Could you do it for two minutes? What about five minutes?

Silence is important for our memory and emotions. According to a 2013 study, it was discovered that silence produces new cells in the hippocampus region of the brain, thus making it larger.[9] The hippocampus is linked to learning, memory, and emotion. It is our "fight or flight" system. It is what allows us to feel and react.

We also know that those diagnosed with depression and high stress levels have a smaller hippocampus. Therefore, if

---

[9] "Is silence golden? Effects of auditory stimuli and their absence on adult hippocampal neurogenesis", Imke Kirste, Zeina Nicola, Golo Kronenberg, Tara L. Walker, Robert C. Liu, and Gerd Kempermann, Published online 2013 Dec 1. doi: 10.1007/s00429-013-0679-3

we can "work out" this portion of our brain, practicing just five minutes of being "mute" every day, we may be better at choosing our emotions in certain situations and reacting in a positive manner to the "moments" that occur in our lives.

So, the first thing I want you to do for five minutes every day is be alone with no distractions, no sound, just you and your thoughts. Make your world MUTE. Turn your phone to silent, shut down your computer, find a room where the dog, cat, or kids are not going to be running around. Eliminate all environmental distractions. Set a timer so that you do not worry about how many minutes you have conquered during the process.

OUTCOME

Stop playing small. You have ONE life. ONE opportunity. Make it count. What is the ONE outcome you want to achieve in life? An outcome that would allow you to look into the eyes of your loved ones if you had only *seven more days* left to live, and say, "It's okay. I did it. I made a difference. I can now leave this earth with no regrets." What is THAT outcome for you?

Make it impactful. Make it influential. Don't settle. Write it down. This becomes your lifetime "achieve anything" goal, your lifetime outcome goal.

I believe my mom's lifetime achieve anything goal was to teach us that we all have good days and bad days, but regardless, they all should be positive days. Our family wrote about this for her eulogy in a piece called, "The Chosen One."

The Chosen One

A letter from Ronda's family – Larry, Jason & Amy

During Ronda's journey with a cancerous brain tumor called glioblastoma multiforme (GBM), we had many approach us and ask about how we were doing, and how we could go on and not question why Ronda was having to go through such a terrible thing such as brain cancer.

Many of you said, "Why does this happen to such a good, nice person such as Ronda?"

We know it would have been easy to question our faith, the world and everyone around us. It would have been easy to complain and question why us, why now, why Ronda?

Here is why we accepted this as we did. You see, we believe Ronda was specifically selected to endure such a nasty diagnosis because she was chosen to deliver a message to all of her friends and family. That message starts with: no matter how bad it seems, you must have a positive attitude no matter what!!! You must accept challenges in life and always know that something good will come from something that we think is bad.

None of us know how long we are to be alive, but those who knew Ronda knew that she made the most out of every day that she was with us on Earth. Many of you who knew her very well may be surprised, but Ronda faced many challenges all her life beginning with being badly burned as a small girl. She had many scars from that time of her life, but never let them get the best of her. She endured many surgeries from knee to shoulder to skin cancer to battles with arthritis. She had hearing deficiencies and struggled with Sjogren's syndrome, a disorder that causes severe dry eyes, dry mouth, and joint pain. Hardly any of you were aware because of Ronda's personality, tenacity, positive attitude, and love for life. She always accepted these life challenges as part of life and made the best of each day. One foot in front of the other and one day at a time. Now that defines and helps you to know what kind of a person she was. I am sure many of you had no idea of some of the challenges Ronda dealt with every day because she was so positive about what a good life she was living.

Therefore, now we can tell you why we believe she was selected to teach so many about how to live life. We have known for years and realized that we, too, were especially blessed to be married to Ronda, to have her as our mother, and we were the recipients of parts of her personality and positive attitude. She never met anyone who didn't become her friend. In her younger years, she was a little shy and had trouble introducing herself to people she didn't know. Once she perfected her introductory skills, she introduced herself to the thousands of friends that she had throughout her life. Many of you here today can attest to being greeted by Ronda with a smile that you will never forget and immediately knowing this was someone who could become a lifelong friend. A higher power had laid out a plan for her, and now we all know why she was selected to endure this lasting hardship.

No matter what was thrown at Ronda, she always wanted to make something good out of it. She especially taught all of us to show appreciation for the care that nurses, therapists, and medical specialists provided. One of Ronda's last wishes was to establish a scholarship in her name dedicated to children of Nebraska County officials who are going into nursing or medical school. That is just one of the positive things that that will be attributed to Ronda as a lasting memorial.

Up to her last breath, she continued to teach us about how to treat people, and it is a lesson that we will carry in our hearts forever. We know that she was placed on this Earth for a reason, and we hope that you now know why she endured this terrible cancer. It was so that she would have time to visit with many of you and teach us all how to die with dignity and grace.

It was so that she could tell many of us to get over ourselves and treat others as we would want to be treated.

It was so that she could show us all that no matter how terrible each day may be, we always say "please" and "thank you." She taught us to always say "thank you" every time a nurse administered a pain medicine or repositioned her. Ronda had a way to even make the nurses feel good when they were having a bad day.

Through all her treatments, surgeries, and recoveries, she always remained positive and said that today is a good day and tomorrow will be better.

Now you know why we feel so blessed to have Ronda as a mother and a wife, and why she was "The Chosen One." We hope that you can all feel the healing power that Ronda has instilled in all of us. We hope that you share her positive attitude as you go through the rest of your life.

We know that going forward, we will have good days and bad days, but we will make them all positive days, just as Ronda taught us.

So, what is your lifetime outcome goal? If your family were to write your eulogy, would it be said that you achieved your lifetime outcome goal? Would it be the legacy that you intended?

I believe that there are two outcome goals you should set for your life: a lifetime outcome goal and a yearly outcome goal.

Remember, these are deep, impactful, influential goals. Do not ever say to yourself as you are trying to identify what your outcome goals are things like:

"That's too big."

"I will never be able to achieve that."

"That is out of my reach."

Instead, say the following out loud (in a mirror if you dare) before you determine what these two outcomes are:

"I was meant for this!"

"I GET to achieve any goal I determine!"

"My time is worth it!"

"I WILL make a difference!"

Now go get it! What is your lifetime outcome goal and yearly outcome goal? Write them down. Do not hesitate. Do not judge.

For your five-minute M.O.M.E.N.T. practice on "Outcome," I want you to determine what you are going to do this day to get you one step closer to both your lifetime outcome and your yearly outcome. Remember this is your "achieve anything" goal. Once you determine what step you are going to take, write it down and commit to taking that one step today that will bring you closer to your goal. It does not matter how small or big the step is, just remember progress will get you there. Perfectionism will halt you.

"The two most important days in your life are the day you are born and the day you find out why."

—**Mark Twain**

MEMORIZE

Remaining positive in all circumstances can be hard. Wouldn't it be great if anytime negativity approached, an automatic fortress sprung up around us to keep out the negativity? We can't have a literal fortress, of course, but there is something we can do to protect ourselves. This brings us to the third practice of M.O.M.E.N.T: Memorize. Specifically, memorize affirmations.

First, let's take a closer look at affirmations.

We can train our brains to combat negativity using self-affirmations. A self-affirmation is a statement about the value of one's self. For example:

- I have the talent to achieve my goals.
- Happiness is a choice, and I choose happiness every day.
- I am valued, confident, and worth it.
- My strengths will allow me to succeed.
- I am superior to negativity.
- My success is limitless.

A word of caution: Always think in the strongest "outcome" language you can possibly use. For example, instead of saying: "I know I can achieve anything I want to achieve." Instead say, "I will achieve anything I want to achieve." See the difference?

Affirmations are "I" statements that you can create for yourself to directly address your own triggers and self-doubt, and the idea is to simply repeat them multiple times. It's a process, and it's not as easy as it sounds! You might simply feel silly chanting to yourself in the mirror. On the other hand, saying things to yourself that you've never heard from others might be a profoundly moving experience: it's different for everybody. If you have never felt worthy of love, for example, telling yourself, "I deserve to be loved" might be very difficult indeed. In fact, the harder a phrase is to say repeatedly, the higher the chance that you are addressing a very deep wound indeed. Therefore, the harder it is to say, the more often you should be saying it, so you can reset a long-established pattern.

For some people, looking themselves in the eye and repeating the affirmations to the mirror is effective. Or you may find writing them down, page after page until your hand aches is the best way. You might also take the Post-It approach and stick affirmations in places where you'll see them every day. Or you could even enlist the help of a loved one, who can offer affirmations from their perspective.

Activity: Affirmations for Beginners

- Reflecting on the work you've done so far, write seven SHORT "I statements." (They must be easy to say!)

- On day one, spend thirty seconds on the first statement, saying it aloud to yourself in the mirror.

- On each subsequent day, spend thirty seconds on the first statement, but add another thirty seconds for the second statement.

- Do the same thing for five more days, adding a new statement each day. By day seven, you'll be spending three-and-a-half minutes on affirmations. It doesn't sound like a long time, but I guarantee you'll find it hard!

Make up your own statements using the following prompts:

I am worthy of _____

I know I can _____

I forgive myself for _____

I endeavor to _____

I accept that _____

I am grateful for _____

I radiate _____

It is not so much what you write down, but the attitude that you take toward your affirmation. In other words, if your thoughts and beliefs around your affirmation are positive, then in turn, you will make positive progress to an improved state of being. Keep it with you all day and occasionally come back to it, giving in to mindfulness a few times during the day.

As you become more adept at affirming yourself, work it into your daily routine. Determine what your self-affirmation is that you are going to carry throughout your day. Write it down, and with whatever time you have remaining of this five-minute practice, **memorize it**, and repeat it out loud, again and again. You are going to memorize it because throughout the day you are going to say it to yourself whenever you think about it. I like to set an alarm on my phone for three different times during the day. When my alarm alerts me, I recite my memorized self-affirmation for that day.

> **"** *There is nothing either good or bad but thinking makes it so.* **"**
>
> —**Shakespeare**

EXPRESS

"I've told her everything I wanted to say." My dad uttered these words in the final days of my mom's life. None of us wanted her to take her last breath while any of us felt regret for anything we may have done or didn't do, said or didn't say. In those eight months from diagnosis to death, my dad, my brother, and I were sure to lay it all on the table for her.

There are many fears in life, and regret is a powerful one. If you had only *seven more days* left to live, would you be harboring any regret? Do you have any friendships that have dwindled over time? Perhaps your own words pierced someone's heart somewhere along this journey of life. Or, maybe you always wanted to share something with someone, but just didn't feel brave enough to do so. In Madonna's words, "Express Yourself!"

On the flip side of that, what if you found out that someone in your life (in your past, present, or even future) had only *seven more days* left to live? Would you have any regret then? What would you do? What would you want to say to them?

During the Parkland, Florida school shooting in February 2018, I read many stories about students sending "goodbye texts" to their families. They were in hiding, not knowing if they would make it out. In those moments, those texts were filled with fear and love. If that was your friend, child, mom, dad, in a situation like that, what would your goodbye text say?

Do that now. Express your feelings or thoughts to a family member, friend, coworker, etc. Write a card, send a text, make a phone call. It does not need to be anything elaborate.

I just received one this morning from my brother that said, "I'm just thinking about the people I am thankful for in my life and wanted to check in on them. What are you most excited about for today?" That was nothing earth-shattering, but I know he cares about me. And if I found myself in a seven-more-days scenario, one thing I would never question is that my brother loves me.

It's that simple.

NOBLE ACT

As defined by the Merriam-Webster dictionary, "noble" is having, showing, or coming from personal qualities that people admire (such as honesty, generosity, courage, etc.).

A 2004 study looked at the relationship between kindness and well-being. Students performed thirty "random acts of kindness" (five per week for six weeks), which were defined as acts that "benefit others or make others happy, typically at some cost to the giver (e.g., cooking a meal for someone, donating blood, helping someone with yard work, or offering your seat to an elderly, disabled or pregnant person)." When compared to those in the control group, who were not required to commit any random acts of kindness, the "kind" students showed an increase in happiness.[10]

Identify an unselfish noble act that you can do today and implement it. It can be for someone you know, or it doesn't have to be. Do not leave it to chance and say, "Oh, I will just do something today as it comes up." Be intentional and identify what it is going to be now. Determine exactly when you are

---

[10] Lyubomirsky, S., Tkach, C., & Yelverton, J. (2004). "Pursuing sustained happiness through random acts of kindness and counting one's blessings: Tests of two six-week interventions," Unpublished data, University of California, Riverside, Department of Psychology.

going to execute and follow through. Noble acts can be as simple as paying for someone else's coffee to sending a package overseas to our soldiers. Here is a list to get your ideas flowing:

1. Give care items to a pet rescue facility.

2. Drop off flowers at a hospital. The hospital will know who needs them the most.

3. Make a meal for your neighbors.

4. Forgive someone, even if they don't ask for it.

5. Pay another child's past-due lunch account balance at your own child's school.

6. Leave a note of kindness on someone's windshield.

7. Help someone load their groceries into their car.

8. Say "Hi" to a stranger and tell them to "Have a great day!"

9. Provide goodie bags for the homeless.

10. Foster a pet to prevent it from being euthanized.

11. Buy fruit and hand it out to homeless people on the street corners on your way into work.

12. Shovel a neighbor's driveway when it snows.

13. Send someone a card in the mail just "because."

14. Put someone else's cart back after shopping.

15. Pay the toll for the car behind you.

16. Pay a portion of the grocery bill for someone who is in line behind you.

17. Buy your new neighbor a batch of return address labels with the new address on them.

18. Bring a coworker breakfast.

19. Hand out a gift card to a police officer, first responder, or soldier in uniform. Look them in their eyes, shake their hand, and say "thank you for your service."

20. Visit a nursing home and talk with the residents.

TERMINATE

This is likely the most difficult of all the practices. What is one thing that you need to eliminate or stop doing to be more positive today? Identify it and terminate it. Do you have somebody in your life who is toxic? Perhaps it's just that jar of M&M's sitting on your desk that may give you instant pleasure for every handful consumed, but leaves you feeling guilty afterward? Are you holding on to a past relationship that just needs to be let go? Today, I want you to take one step closer to eliminating that from your life.

If you want to fill your life with more positivity, then you must make room for it. Do not let negativity or negative environmental stimulus take up that room. You choose how you want to live your day. You choose what you need to terminate for this day so that tomorrow is a better day, so that next week is a better week, so that this year is your best year—so that this life is your best life!

There are no second chances. If you had only *seven more days* left to live, how would you finish these sentences?

- I wish I had not (what)
- I wish I had not let (who) control my life.

- I wish I had never allowed myself to feel (what)

Start there and eliminate those answers from your life, starting today.

Now that we've been through each aspect of M.O.M.E.N.T, let's review the entire system again:

- **M - Mute:** Be silent for five minutes with zero distractions.
- **O - Outcome:** Write down one outcome you must conquer today that will get you one step closer toward your "achieve anything" goal.
- **M - Memorize:** Identify and write down your daily phrase for today. Memorize it. Repeat it.
- **E - Express:** Express your feelings to a loved one.
- **N - Noble Act:** Identify an unselfish noble act that you can do for someone today and implement it.
- **T - Terminate:** Terminate one thing in your life that is not bringing you positivity.

Need more inspiration to get started? Here are what others who have come before you said about implementing the M.O.M.E.N.T. practices into their lives.

"The biggest result I saw, or shall I say felt, was how freeing it was to let go of those things or people that no longer serve me in a positive direction or my ultimate goal. My plan is to continue the M.O.M.E.N.T. practice. I know there is always room for improvement in myself." —Amy L.

"During my trial run, I was in Texas on a business trip. In what should have been a hectic and potentially a very stressful trip, was surprisingly calm and relaxing. Being able to just take a few minutes out of each day to just be one with yourself and reflect on where you were, where you are, where you're going; it's a great feeling. This is a practice I plan to continue using and also pass along to family and friends so that they too can find peace within themselves." —Dustin W.

"I saw immediate results from the Acts of Kindness. These are things I do from time to time now, but when I was thinking about it on a daily basis, it made life more fun

and exciting trying to create those moments each day . . . when I took my daily routine and added a new, creative twist on it (the MOMENTS), life got more fun and interesting and it kept it fresh, I loved it." —Joel P.

"I think having a daily practice of this nature helps you be calm in moments of stress and focus on the good that is always around you. I felt very uplifted and joyous and look forward to continuing the practice!" —Lindi F.

"I enjoyed it. I appreciated taking the time to be totally alone for a few minutes. I felt better at the end of the day because I interacted with all kinds of people and made sure that I spent time listening to them and hearing them, and also by complimenting people you could see them light up." —Mary Ann G.

Activity: Worksheet

Visit www.thepositivelifeco.com/seven-more-days and download the following worksheet entitled: M.O.M.E.N.T. Daily Practice Form.

M.O.M.E.N.T. DAILY PRACTICE FORM

❏ MUTE
Be silent for 5 minutes with absolutely zero distractions.

❏ OUTCOME
Write down one outcome that you must conquer today that will get you one step closer towards your "achieve anything" goal.

My Lifetime Achieve Anything Goal is: _____

The action I will take today to get me one step closer to Lifetime Achieve Anything goal

will be:_____

❏ MEMORIZE
Identify and write down your daily phrase for today. Memorize it. Repeat it.

My self-affirmation for today is:_____

❏ EXPRESS
Express your feelings to a loved one.

The person I am going to express my thoughts or feelings to is:_____

I am going to do that by (how will you communicate it - ie: card, text, etc):_____

❏ NOBLE ACT
Identify a unselfish noble act that you can do for someone today and implement it.

The noble act that I am going to perform today is: _____

❏ TERMINATE
Terminate one thing in your life that is not bringing you positivity.

The thing that I am going to eliminate from my life today is: _____

The M.O.M.E.N.T. practices will transform your life, but what happens when you have a moment that was less than positive and/or had a negative effect on your day? This is where the L.U.C.Y. circle comes in.

I Love L.U.C.Y

The L.U.C.Y circle is a super-simple system that is going to help you to instantly and effortlessly live a more positive life. It's not necessarily something you do "in the moment," but rather something you can do as you mull over the day's or week's events.

L.U.C.Y is not just a random acronym; it's the name my mom liked to go by. Her middle name was "Lou," but she loved the name Lucy, and even wanted to legally change her name to Lucy before she passed away. She couldn't do that, but her headstone honors that preference and reads "Ronda 'Lucy.'"

Happily, the letters of "Lucy" lend themselves perfectly to my purpose here.

L.U.C.Y stands for:

- **L - LOOK**
- **U - UNDERSTAND**
- **C - CHALLENGE**
- **Y - YOU**

And it looks like this:

Now let's break it down.

LOOK

The first stage of the circle is all about looking for an opportunity to be more positive. This doesn't mean you should invent scenarios in which you can be more positive; rather, you should be taking advantage of the opportunities that naturally present themselves, almost daily, which leave you with a negative emotion.

This stage is simply about observation without judgment: *What was the situation and what did you feel?*

Perhaps it's something small, such as being kept waiting too long in line for coffee because someone dithered over their order. Maybe you felt your blood pressure rising with frustration. Maybe you entertained uncharitable thoughts about the person holding up everyone's day. Maybe you expressed your irritation by snapping at the person on the other side of the counter when it was finally your turn to place your order.

Or the incident might be something much more significant. Perhaps the workplace rumor mill was churning out fear of redundancies again today. Perhaps you were too distracted by anger to get much done, or perhaps you even thought about who might be plotting to throw you under the bus to save themselves, wondering whether you should take some preemptive action before they get the chance to succeed.

These are two examples from the everyday-problem spectrum of life, but if there's one thing we can be sure of: something will happen during the course of twenty-four hours that will cause a hot flash of negativity. But it's important to acknowledge these things without judgment of ourselves because, as mere humans, our first thoughts about a difficult situation are often pretty dark. Think about the time you felt a jolt of glee on discovering someone you didn't like got fired or befell some other catastrophe. Hey, we've all been there. But the best of us don't allow our first thoughts to stick around longer than a few seconds, abandoning them in favor of something less reactionary, something perhaps more compassionate. So, if you responded badly to something in the heat of the moment, simply observe that behavior and move on to the next stage in the L.U.C.Y Circle.

UNDERSTAND

Recognize your behavior is important, but now it's time to understand it. Again, without judgment.

Why were you annoyed about being kept waiting in line too long for your morning coffee? Was it something specific, such as having overslept that morning and being worried about getting to work late? Or was it a broader issue, such as being a generally impatient person who wants everything five minutes ago?

When we experience negative emotions, these are needs that are not being met. For example, if you are not invited to a friend's gathering and you feel hurt by that, then your need of feeling connected is not being met. Conversely, when you feel positive emotions, your needs are being met. For example, if you post an article on LinkedIn that you are proud of, then your needs of fulfillment and ego are being satisfied.

You are doing this for yourself, so be as honest as you can, even if you don't like the answer to your questions. The more often you practice this circle, the more behavior patterns will emerge and the better equipped you will be to address them. We'll discuss these negativity "triggers" in more detail in Chapter 5, but being aware of the day-to-day aggravations will give you a list of things to work on. We're always a work in progress!

CHALLENGE

At this point in the circle, this process gets difficult. This is the point at which you challenge the response you had and think about the ways you could have handled it.

If you are having trouble determining how else you could have handled a situation, simply use the strategy of opposite thinking. For example, if you snapped at someone, what is the opposite of that? Saying something kind. If you sighed loudly in annoyance, next time practice calming, mindful breathwork. If you feel bad about having engaged in an unkind conversation about someone, in future you could reach out to the person being gossiped about to check whether they are okay.

Try writing down your negative action and your ideas for a positive reaction for the next time the situation arises. And there may be more than one idea for a better response to the problem: the more the merrier because the more options you'll have the next time.

YOU (Apply)

The final quarter of the circle is about how you apply the change. It may not always be possible to apply your new behavior immediately, but you will be prepared for the next time the situation arises.

The beauty of a circle is that you'll always return to the beginning where you have the opportunity to do something differently. Taking the learning from the "challenge" phase, you can apply the lesson. But if you're worried you may not get the chance to apply your learning again, you can backtrack by taking the situation into your own hands. For example, if you wonder whether you upset someone or let them down, send them a note to say sorry. Sometimes that person won't have a clue what you're apologizing for! Perhaps they weren't as affected by your actions as you imagined; nevertheless, I can almost guarantee that he or she will be touched that you reached out.

By putting in the energy into rectifying a situation, or by being inconvenienced by the effort, you're less likely to make the same mistake again.

> **"***It is the highest form of self-respect to admit our errors and mistakes and make amends for them.* **"**
>
> —**Dale E. Turner, American actor**

L.U.C.Y is simply a way to take a more methodical approach to building your positivity. It may not suit everybody, but it's a good tool to try out, at least a few times. The more times you go around the circle, the easier it will get, and the more ingrained it will become as a thought pattern. And although you'll probably find yourself going around in L.U.C.Y circles quite often at first, this frequency will diminish as you become more adept at applying positivity in your everyday life. But the truth is that circles have no end and, probably, your quest for positivity will have no end because there'll be new, unexpected challenges coming at you every day that will force you to reflect upon your response to negativity.

So, here we are at the end of Part One. For the remainder of the book, we're going to explore the three pillars of positivity, which are inspired by my mom's life. By observing and analyzing her life, I came to the realization that the secret lies in the mastery of three Cs:

1. Character
2. Connections
3. Community

There is a reason the three Cs are numbered: building positivity comes in stages. Character comes first; this is our foundation and our glue. Once we have begun to work on ourselves, we can then make better connections with our inner circle of friends, family, coworkers, and regular acquaintances. Then, as we improve our closest relationships, we can better engage with an outer circle of people to become better members of a wider community—a community which might be local, national, or even global! Just imagine being able to inspire positivity and happiness on the other side of the world; how fulfilled would you be then?

> **"**_Each morning when I open my eyes I say to myself: I, not events, have the power to make me happy or unhappy today. I can choose which it shall be. Yesterday is dead, tomorrow hasn't arrived yet. I have just one day, today, and I'm going to be happy in it._ **"**
>
> **—Groucho Marx, American comic**

Part Two:

Character

In March of 2017, I could not shake the number 1210. It was everywhere. I would see it almost daily on clocks, on my watch, on signs, on receipts, in the airport—everywhere! Around that time, I was home in Lincoln, Nebraska. While there, I decided to visit my mom's work to visit with her past coworkers, who were so supportive while my mom was dying. As soon as I walked into the "Communications Building" of EyeCare Specialties (where my mom worked), I suddenly remembered the last time I was there.

It was in the fall of 2015; I flew home to surprise my mom. Since it was a surprise, my mom didn't know to switch her Thursday night shift at the EyeCare Specialties where she was working in the communications department. My dad (Larry) and I decided to visit her that night just to hang out and help pass the time until she got off work. She was the only one working and the phones which she had to answer were sure to be slow. We went into the break room for a snack, and when my mom said she wanted to use the restroom, I asked her what I should do if the phone rang while she was gone. She said, "Let's just hope that doesn't happen!" With that response, my dad and I looked at each other and, as soon as she went into the restroom, we called the main line from one of our cell phones. We heard her from the restroom: "Well, dang!" she exclaimed, and she scrambled out of the restroom and rushed to the phone to discover a dead line. My dad and I fell apart laughing, and my mom said, as she always did: "I'm just here for your entertainment!"

My mom adored working at EyeCare Specialties and made strong bonds there with her coworkers. The employees of EyeCare Specialties were not just my mom's coworkers; they were some of the best friends she could have ever asked for. These friends showed up in my mom's hospital room every week to update her on what was going on at work, their kids, their dogs, and any other topic of conversation you might have if you were simply having a conversation with one of your friends.

While standing next to my mom's old desk on that trip home in March, I couldn't help but think that these "coworkers" may have lost a fellow employee on March 30 of that year, which was the last day my mom worked before going to the Emergency Room on that day for signs of exhaustion, forgetfulness, and trouble walking, but they lost a "friend" on December 10 (12-10), the day my mom took her last breath. Once again, the number 1210 wouldn't escape me.

Not only was it my mom's death date, 12/10 is the birthday of my four-legged child, Sadie Mae, whom my mom absolutely loved. It is also the address of my first home as a child (1210 East 33rd Street, Kearney, NE).

After my mom passed, my brother and I stood in the hospice room with my mom's cold, lifeless body lying on the bed. Tears streaming down his face and a lump in his throat, my brother looked over at my mom and said, "Mom, my first memories of you were at 1210 and my last is on 12/10."

Curious about this number, I sat in Starbucks that day after visiting my mom's work, and googled: "What does the number 1210 mean?" What came up on that search took my breath away!

Ever heard of angel numbers? It is a form of symbology that ascribes numbers to "guardian angels," a belief put forward by author Doreen Virtue in her 2005 book *Angel Numbers 101*.[11] Whether or not you share such spiritual beliefs, you can't deny the wonderful words that describe Angel 1210, taken here from Joanne Walmsley's Sacred Scribes blog:[12]

"Angel Number 1210 is a message from your angels to ensure that what you put out to the Universe is of a positive nature. You are asked to stay on a positive path and to use your natural skills, talents, and abilities to their utmost for the benefit of yourself and others ... Angel Number 1210 is a message to stay positive."

I like to believe that my mom was guarded by Angel 1210, and that now I can help spread that angel's message even further.

In Part Two, we focus in on ourselves and examine the qualities we possess that we can leverage for greater positivity. This will allow you to discover (1) who you are, (2) how you view others, and (3) how you view the world. When you can understand the

---

[11] Doreen Virture, Angel Numbers 101 (Carlsbad: Hay House Publishing, 2008)

[12] http://sacredscribesangelnumbers.blogspot.com.au/2012/09/angel-number-1210.html (September 19, 2012). Accessed April 2018.

simple psychology behind these three things, you can begin to live a life of complete fulfillment, joy, and positivity, and you will empower your own life and other people's.

Chapter 4

Who Do You Think You Are?

To live a life of fulfillment, we have to understand who we are, first. But when was the last time you stopped to think about that? And how is it even possible to think objectively about your own character?

Spunky. When asked for one word to describe my mom, that was the response I received more than any other word. When my mom was in the hospital, I thought a great self-esteem booster would be to design a "character" word cloud for my mom. If you are unfamiliar with a word cloud, it is an image compilation of words that refer to a single subject, in which the size of each word indicates the frequency of its repetition. The more often a word is referred to, the bigger that word appears in the word cloud. I took to social media and asked, "What is one word you would use to describe Ronda?" The responses flooded in. After hundreds of submissions, I created my mom's character word cloud, pictured here.

I remember the framed word cloud poster eventually found its spot on the wall hanging above her bed in hospice. Standing at the foot of her bed, looking at her, then looking at the word cloud, I asked, "Spunky. Do you feel like that describes you well, Mom?"

"I sure do!" she replied.

Other prominent words that stand out on her poster where others describe her character include caring, fun, and (of course) POSITIVE!

What a true testament to her character. If you had only *seven more days* left to live and were to ask others to describe you in one word, how would your word cloud turn out?

The older we get, the more we tend to take who we are for granted. We might even say, "Can't teach an old dog new tricks," or "A leopard can't change its spots." But these sayings cast us as victims of the aging process or our past upbringing. They ignore the fact that throughout our lives, we are on a journey that teaches us new lessons almost every day and underplay our ability to learn and grow continuously.

In the simplest terms, who we are is made up of two things:

- Personality
- Behaviors

If you've ever done something you're ashamed of, you'll know that these two components can be very distinct. When we feel shame, we're experiencing a disconnect between our personality and our behavior: the shame tells us we did something out of character.

The bad news is that your personality is somewhat fixed. It forms early in life and provides a set of parameters for your world. The good news is that our behaviors are more within our control, and with practice, behaviors help soften those hard edges of our core personality.

Here's something from my own experience to illustrate this point. In my early days as a manager at a $1 billion company, I would be quite judgmental while interviewing people. When my boss would ask, "What do you think?" I would rattle off at least ten reasons why that person would not be good, would not be qualified, or just reasons why I didn't like them. I remember one day, my boss saying to me, "Amy, this position is a hard position to fill with a small pool of qualified candidates. Why don't you tell me what you think was good about this person, and let's see if we can build him up to be the employee that we want him to be."

Wow! I had been schooled. That experience revealed my core personality and the behavior I should adopt to overcome that negativity. That man was a true leader. He taught me to see the good in people and amplify their *strengths*. We all have weaknesses, and sometimes they can be changed, but our strengths are what make us the amazing individuals that we are. It takes a lot less effort to capitalize on our strengths than to try to change our weaknesses.

If you've not been in the habit of reflecting on yourself recently, I'd like to offer a few painless ways to view your personality without necessitating an expensive trip to a therapist.

A Novel Approach

First, think about which novel you would like to have with you if you're ever stranded on a desert island: it would be the only book you ever get to read again, so make it a good one! Is it a modern thriller? Or a nineteenth-century melodrama? Or a fantastical sci-fi adventure?

Whether you enjoy an action-packed page-turner or a gentler, more literary story, the chances are you connected with the book's protagonist—the main character who drags us (or whom we willingly follow) through the narrative. You may love or even hate that character, but you feel something for them: they're people worth writing about.

This is where we think about who we are as the protagonists of our own lives, the story we are living every day. Just as the characters in the books we love are memorable to us, the more we refine our characters, the more positive our impact on others will be. If you were a character in a book, would you be a hero or a villain? Are you the protagonist in your own life? Or are you a caricature who is buffeted by events all around them and a victim to the actions of others?

In creative writing, the consensus among authors of quality is that "good" characters (the ones that hold us captivated) should have complexity that makes them interesting; flaws that make them identifiable; fears and desires that make them sympathetic; and a strong voice that helps us see the world in a different way. These are the obvious qualities, and I'm sure you—as real people—have these too. But there are a few less obvious qualities left to highlight.

Strong, likeable (or sympathetic), and heroic literary characters have these qualities, too:

- **Agency:** Someone who has power over his or her own life and events
- **Room for growth:** Someone who is becoming a better person and overcoming personal obstacles
- **Connections to others:** Someone who is not a loner, who has fulfilling relationships and helps others through friendship

Do you have agency? Do you feel in control of your life story? This is a key issue when it comes to your ability to be positive because, when we feel our lives are being dictated to by other people or circumstances, it's hard to maintain a sunny outlook. Society has certain expectations of you, and it's easy to get into a situation in which you are living a life for others, rather than yourself. When you carry the pressures and the expectations of society on your shoulders, you will never be able to live your best life because you are constantly spending too much energy caring about what others think and trying to live up to their expectations. To have agency means living up to *your own* expectations. It is not up to society or others whether you are a good person. At the end of the day, only you have to know that you are a good person and that you're following your passion. Nobody gets to tell you what your passions are. And when you make steps to follow your own passion, then you can't help but to live with agency.

Do you have humility? Can you accept that you still have some personal development to do? Some of the most unhappy, negative people I know are those who believe that they're right all the time (and everybody else is an idiot); they live in fear of failing and in a permanent state of outrage or irritation! Think about the last time you learned a new skill, experienced something for the first time, or challenged yourself to listen to a different point of view. I'll bet you felt great about it, so my advice is to do more of it!

And what about your impact on others? Do people seek your company? We'll talk more about connections in Part Three, but hopefully, as you think about yourself more, you'll think about yourself in relation to others, too.

The Jungian Approach

The other way to look more objectively at yourself is through the lens of the "personality archetype," which is a notion that comes to us from Swiss psychologist Carl Jung (1875–1961).[13] Archetype means "original pattern," and so it suggests that we all conform to molds, which some may not like the thought of. But throughout my business research (carried out when we help entrepreneurs build high-end businesses based on psychology), I've found these archetypes to be fairly accurate.

Although we are all unique beings, we possess certain innate qualities deep in our core that are not learned. Carl Jung determined that our psyches possess subconscious characteristics that are in place, even before any outside influences come into play. I like to explain it as our core personality type. You don't get to choose. Jung suggests that you were born with it, and according to him, there are twelve archetypes. However, I believe that the archetypes can be fitted into four categories, which help determine the ultimate outcome that you want to achieve in life.

---

[13] C. G. Jung (translated by R.F.C. Hull), *The Archetypes and The Collective Unconscious (Collected Works of C.G. Jung Vol.9 Part 1)*, (Princeton, NJ: Princeton University Press, 1981)

Activity: Determine Your Archetype

It's simple to determine your archetype by answering two questions.

Question 1: What is your ultimate goal in life? (Choose ONE)

1. Be Extraordinary
2. Live Your Dreams
3. Change the World
4. Connect with Others

Question 2: What is your GREATEST aspiration? (Find your number from Question 1 and then choose the letter that best describes your aspiration under that number)

1. Be Extraordinary
   a) Care for or help others
   b) Solve a problem through the creation of a product or service
   c) Be viewed as massively successful

2. Live Your Dreams
   d) Live a fulfilling and authentic life
   e) Live a simple life
   f) Live a better life through knowledge

3. Change the World
    g) Overcome challenges to save the world
    h) Make the impossible possible
    i) Conquer by unconformity

4. Connect with Others
    j) Have a good time and laugh
    k) Experience a deep connection through love
    l) Fit in and find friends

After answering these two questions, you should have a number and a letter. Match your number and letter combination with your archetype below. For example, if you answered that your ultimate goal is to be extraordinary (category 1) and that your greatest aspiration is to care for and help others (item a.), your combination is 1a, or The Caregiver.

The Personality Types

Be Extraordinary	Live Your Dreams
1a) The Caregiver	2d) The Explorer
1b) The Creator	2e) The Innocent
1c) The Ruler	2f) The Sage
Change the World	**Connect with Others**
3g) The Hero	4j) The Jester
3h) The Magician	4k) The Lover
3i) The Outlaw/Rebel	4l) The Regular Guy/Gal

This graphic will help you position yourself within this archetype structure. Are you surprised by the outcome? Do you agree with it? More importantly, are you happy with that outcome? Personality is hard to change, but you could incorporate the more favorable characteristics of other archetypes by adapting your behaviors.

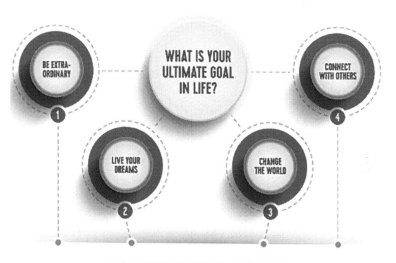

WHAT IS YOUR GREATEST ASPIRATION?

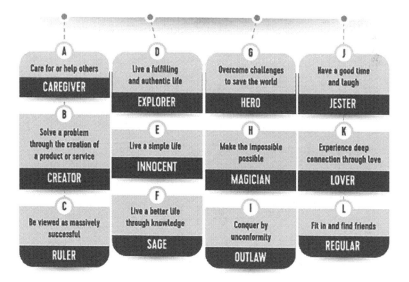

Knowing your archetype gives you a sense of the potential barriers you need to overcome to change your behaviors. Here is some insight into what issues each archetype might encounter:

Archetype	Positives	Challenges
Caregiver	Nurturing, Caring, Gentle, Mother-Like, Grateful	Can be taken advantage of. Finds it hard to say no.
Creator	Creative, Self-Expression, Innovative	So focused on quality that sometimes won't finish a product. Perfectionist.
Ruler	Perfectionist, Organized	Controlling. Has a hard time delegating.
Explorer	Adventurer, Trailblazer, Freedom-Seeking	Wants everything on own terms. No real direction.
Innocent	Positive, Simple, Pure	Can be viewed as boring. May be indecisive.
Sage	Data-Driven, Expert	Always wanting to know more, so has a hard time taking action. Can be hard to relate to at times.

Hero	Brave, Courageous, Motivational, Determined	Vain, pushy, controlling.
Magician	Persistent, Life-Changing, Makes Things Happen	Manipulative, controlling
Outlaw/Rebel	Determined, Edgy	Can be feared. Rebellious.
Outlaw/Rebel	Determined, Edgy	Can be feared. Rebellious.
Jester	Likes to Entertain, Fun-Loving, Dynamic	Senseless, foolish.
Lover	Sensual, Elegant	Always wanting to please others, so has a hard time standing up for own self.
Regular guy/ gal	Relatable, Engaging, Charismatic, Friendly	Loses identity for the sake of blending in.

Be aware of the disadvantages so that your personality type does not hold you back from living life as positively as you can. My mom did this archetype test. She was super skeptical about the notion of archetypes, but excited to take the test anyway. Her result came back as "regular gal," which might have disappointed some people (we all tend to believe our characters are grander than they really are), but my mom was jubilant. She said, "Yep! That's me all right—a regular gal.

That's why I'm such a great friend to people!" She was correct. She was a great friend to people, and she was very self-aware of her strengths (positives) and her challenges.

If you're still having trouble thinking about your character, I recommend taking the psychometric character strengths personality test offered by the VIA Institute on Character.[14] The survey recognizes twenty-four character strengths that are put into six categories: Wisdom, Courage, Humanity, Justice, Temperance, and Transcendence. The Institute believes that by identifying and playing to your character strengths, you can "buffer against, manage, and overcome problems," "improve your relationships," and "enhance your health and overall well-being." The Institute's website also has a lot of useful information about what to do with your newfound knowledge of your character strengths.

Effect of Your Genes

So, where did the personality type we're stuck with come from? The answer may be in your genes.

I believe that the positivity gene on my mom's side of the family must be strong, because she held on to her happiness despite some terrible trauma, including losing her grandmother, mother, and both of her brothers to pancreatic cancer. Rather than letting each successive loss erode her positivity, she seemed to have augmented it.

---

[14] https://www.viacharacter.org/survey/account/register

I got my positivity from my mom, and I'm sure it's an issue of nature rather than nurture because we also had some fundamental differences. Both super high-energy, we would get excited about even the smallest things in life and show how jazzed we were to the world. We both understood that, even when you're tired or sick, showing enthusiasm helps change your entire demeanor and the situation. But I don't share my mom's impulsivity. If she liked the look of something, she'd buy it; if something sounded fun, she would just go out and do it. I have too much of a business brain, and it holds me back from doing things on a whim; I am more analytical. My mom went with the flow and was content to let my dad make most decisions, which worked for her. If you asked her, "Hey, where do you want to eat tonight?" she would reply, "Somebody else just tell me, and I'll be there. I'll bring the fun." And she always did. (Oh, and the one other thing we shared was we were "boy crazy" in our youth. Mom assured me I got that from her!)

The Science of Happiness

During one of my last visits to my mom, I had a list of questions I wanted to ask her. I had realized that she was diminishing quickly, and I thought that if I wanted to learn anything from her, my window of time was also diminishing. As I sat in her hospice room holding her hand, I looked at my questions and asked her the first one on my list (I still don't remember what it was to this day), but I quickly realized there was not going to be any real conversation with her; she found it too difficult to put thoughts and sentences together. I scanned the list of questions again and selected just one: "Mom, how can others live a life a positivity like you have?" In a meek, matter-of-fact voice, while holding my hand, she whispered, "I don't know. I believe either you are positive, or you aren't." This was one of the last full sentences she ever said that was directed to just me, and it became the basis of my research for The Positive Life Company. I wondered, "Was she on to something? Are we born positive or can it be learned?"

In a 2005 research project by the University of California, Riverside, entitled, "Pursuing Happiness: The Architecture of Sustainable Change,"[15] researcher Sonja Lyubomirsky suggests that happiness is influenced by three factors:

1. **Genes:** 50 percent
2. **Activities:** 40 percent
3. **Environment:** 10 percent

This means that, broadly speaking, if you consider yourself unhappy with your life, changing your environment (e.g., moving to a new place) will have the least effect. Intentionally changing the way you live (new activities) will be more effective, but you're fighting the biggest fight with your own genes. And if you're genetically predisposed to negativity, you're having to fight particularly hard.

Another research project, published in 2015, with the catchy title, "Neurogenetic Variations in Norepinephrine Availability

---

[15] Sonja Lyubomirsky & Kennon M. Sheldon, "Pursuing Happiness: The Architecture of Sustainable Change," (*Review of General Psychology,* 2005. Vol. 9, No. 2, 111-131)

Enhance Perceptual Vividness,"[16] explores the genes that are responsible for how we perceive events through our emotions. The researchers looked at the "ADRA2b gene deletion variant," which regulates the neurotransmitter norepinephrine. Carriers of the gene variant experience "enhanced emotional vividness," i.e., a greater response to the threats and rewards of life. It is suggested that ethnicity may be a factor in whether you carry the gene variant, and it's estimated that 50% of Caucasians are carriers. Carriers are more prone to seeing the world in more extreme emotional ways. Obviously, this is important because the vividness with which we perceive events has an impact on our mental and physical well-being. We can conclude from this that people view the world differently. Indeed, your friend can experience the same situation as you, but look at it differently. If your friend is a carrier of the variant and perceives an event as negative, he or she will believe it is an extremely negative occurrence, whereas you may just think it is a neutral event.

What's Your Positivity Baseline?

So, we've looked at the fundamentals of character and the underlying science behind who you are. Clearly, there is a wealth of detailed psychology data that falls outside the scope of this book, which you can explore at a later stage; but for now, we can conclude this chapter by placing ourselves on a positivity spectrum.

---

[16] "Neurogenetic Variations in Norepinephrine Availability Enhance Perceptual Vividness," J Neurosci. 2015 Apr 22;35(16):6506-16. doi: 10.1523/JNEUROSCI.4489-14.2015

Why is it important to know where you sit on the spectrum right now? It will give you a "baseline," from which you can measure your progress over time. By testing yourself now, you'll be able to revisit the test in a year's time and know whether you've shifted your positivity in the right direction.

It's activity time!

Activity: Positivity Assessment

The following assessment sheet can be downloaded at: www.thepositivelifeco.com/seven-more-days

GENERAL POSITIVITY BASELINE ASSESSMENT

1. In general, I consider myself:

1	2	3	4	5	6	7
Not a very positive person						A very positive person

2. Compared to most of my friends, I consider myself:

1	2	3	4	5	6	7
Less Positive						More Positive

3. Some people are generally very positive. They enjoy life regardless of what is happening. To what extent does this describe you?

1	2	3	4	5	6	7
Not at all						A great deal

4. Some people are generally not very positive. They tend to see the challenges in most situations. To what extent does this describe you?

1	2	3	4	5	6	7
A great deal						Not at all

Total Score:_____

Average Score (Total Score /4): _____

1	2	3	4	5	6	7
Need additional support toward a more positive life			Need to refine my living toward a more positive lifestyle			Need to continue living a positive life

If you find yourself faced with a negative baseline, please don't despair! The very last thing I want you to do is feel defeated by that result. Rather, you should be relieved that you've picked up this book! You are taking control, you're gaining the agency we talked about earlier, to change things around by altering your behaviors.

The good news is that you can change the neurological pathways in your brain to be a more positive person. Your brain is a muscle; it must be worked out. By changing your thinking, you're working that muscle. It's just like working out in the gym, where if you exercise for thirty days straight, you will change the composition of your body. The same idea applies with your brain: If you work it out, you will change its composition.

Have you ever had this happen to you? You have a favorite app on your phone. Every time you go to your screen, you automatically know where that app is without even having to study your screen; your finger just goes right to it. Now, you download a new app, and the position of your favorite app changes. The first several times you want to open your favorite app, you tap the wrong one because your muscle memory has been set. You must change your muscle memory to remember its new location on your screen, which is done by the act of repetition. Muscle memory is affected by a fatty tissue in our brains called myelin. When your myelin increases, your muscle memory becomes faster.

Muscle memory is important to positivity too. The more you practice it, the more adept your brain will be at processing the positive emotions and thoughts, until it becomes second nature.

> **❝*Any man could, if he were so inclined, be the sculptor of his own brain.* ❞**
>
> **- Santiago Ramón y Cajal, Spanish pathologist (1852-1934)**

Chapter 5

Building Positive Character

Now that we've got a better sense of who we are, let's begin the work of changing our outlook and improving on our positivity baseline. There are three cornerstones to this process:

- Accept and expect
- Identify negativity triggers
- Self-esteem

One: Accept and Expect

"*Positive feelings come from being honest about yourself and accepting your personality, and physical characteristics, warts and all.* **"**

—**Willard Scott, American author and broadcaster**

It's important to accept where you are on your positivity journey and expect the results accordingly. If you're being the best you can be at any given time, then expect the results you are hoping for will come in time.

Throughout her life, my mom was able to accept who she was and where she was in her life. She didn't dwell on her shyness or discomfort around crowds and strangers, instead she embraced her strengths of being an amazing friend, of always making others feel included. When she would meet someone new, they were instant friends, and she was able to positively impact many lives that way. If she had just focused on her weaknesses and tried to build herself up to be an extrovert, she would have never succeeded. Only by focusing on your strengths can you soar to greater heights.

The journey to better positivity can certainly be frustrating. Some days it might feel as if the universe is testing you every single minute, daring you to be a Debbie/Donnie Downer. Having bad days is a fact of life, so please—for your sanity— just accept them and move on. Living a positive life does not mean that life will become all roses and candy. But the secret to accepting a bad day is changing your expectation of outcomes. If you don't change your expectations and you choose to stay in a state of negativity, then you will never really understand why others don't want to be around you.

When my mom was diagnosed with grade 4 brain cancer, my brother, my dad, and I all knew what the ultimate outcome was going to be, and that we only had a short period of time left with her. We had two options: (1) We could choose to sit in the spin-cycle of negativity, be sad, and have everyone around us be sad, torturing ourselves with unanswerable questions such as *Why does cancer exist? Why does it happen to good people?* Or we could choose option (2), which was to accept the situation for what it was and make the most of the time she had left. We changed our expectations and the desired outcome. If we couldn't save my mom's life, we would make what was left of it the best it could be.

I believe my mom felt this way, too, when it came to her death. First, she had to accept it before she could set her expectations. It appeared she accepted it almost instantly—a great character trait to possess when it comes to positivity.

There is often an eerie coldness to Intensive Care Units (ICU). There are no smiles, no interactions with the other families walking in the hallway—almost a silence on the floor. The main sound on the ICU floor—the rhythmic hiss of sssssssss . . . hoooooo . . . sssssssss . . . hoooooo—comes from the breathing machines that the patients are hooked up to. My mom had been in a coma for over a week after her initial surgery of removing her brain tumor. This day was the first day since "waking up" that she was able to speak. Although she still slept the majority of the time, she would wake up for short moments, oftentimes saying something witty, and then falling back asleep. It was always hard leaving her at night when she was hooked up to all those machines and monitors, so I would stay as long as I could until I knew she was asleep for the night.

One night was particularly emotional. All her visitors had left for the day. My dad and I were the only ones left as the skies turned dark and the night began. He walked out of her ICU room that night, and just before he crossed into the hallway, he turned around, looked at me, and said, "I know it's hard, but you can't stay all night. You need to go home and get some rest."

I knew he was right, but hoped he was wrong. Everything seemed so fragile at that point. It seemed as if, even though my mom was no longer in a coma, her last breath could come at any point, and I just wasn't ready to leave her yet. So, I stood next to her bed, holding her hand, thinking, crying, talking to her with no response as she was in a deep sleep.

Finally, I decided my dad was right. I needed to go home to get some sleep, so I could come back to her room the next day and do it all again. As I started to walk out of her room that night with only the sound of the sssssssss . . . hoooooo . . . sssssssss . . . hoooooo in the background, I was interrupted by my mom's weak voice: "Is it cancer?" she asked. Not prepared for that question, I stalled, and before I could answer, she asked, "Have you contacted hospice yet?"

"Hospice!" I exclaimed. "Oh Mom, I don't think we are there at this point."

She replied, "Make sure your dad calls hospice." It's like she knew. She knew immediately. But no one had even told her diagnosis yet. I didn't even have a chance to confirm her original question. I believe that before she ever went into surgery, she had already accepted that this tumor could be cancer. You see, because she had already accepted it, she wanted to set her expectations accordingly.

The next night, the same scenario played out. She waited until everyone left, woke up and asked me, "How long do I have?"

"Oh Mom! I don't know. I don't think anyone knows."

That was a lie, and we both knew it. I felt she knew that I knew but just wasn't telling her. She was right. I knew the answer to her question. I could have given her a more definitive response. After all, one does not have to google "glioblastoma life expectancy" for very long to know that the average lifespan is about twelve months. With a lump in her throat and a shaky voice, she just said, "Okay."

We both cried and just looked at each other. Finally, she gave in, closed her eyes, and fell asleep. I whispered, "I love you" and left her ICU room for the night. Sssssssss . . . hoooooo . . . sssssssss . . . hoooooo.

I cried the entire way home until I got to the driveway, pulled myself together, and walked inside. I wished I were stronger in that moment to tell her what I knew. Because she had already accepted her fate, she just wanted to be able to accept her expectations, too. In that moment, I wasn't ready to be the one to give them to her.

Of course, it is not easy. It might be the hardest thing you ever have to do, but the more difficult that acceptance is and the harder it is to change your expectations for your desired outcome, the greater the victory you will have won over the dark power of negativity.

It Is What It Is

What we think of as "good" or "bad" in a situation is deeply subjective. One person may find something horrible, yet another will like it. It's personal. So, to help find our inner peace, we have to learn to let go of notions of good or bad, and accept that a situation simply "is."

Think of life like a battery, which needs a negative and positive end. You cannot have the good without the bad, but you must choose what kind of energy your life will be powered by.

But the "it is what it is" attitude doesn't mean tolerating everything and becoming a doormat. What it means is finding the strength to endure an unpleasant event, learn from it, and then let it go. The danger of clinging to negative past experiences is clear: the accumulation will devastate you and tarnish your perception of your past, keeping you stuck in the present and spoiling the life you have left to live. Our minds and bodies can store debilitating experiences and feelings for long periods of time, but it's not good for them. The booming therapy industry can attest to this! Just like toxins in the body, we need to excrete our negativity if we are to be healthy, mentally and physically.

Of course, letting go is easy in theory. In reality, it can be hard because some negativity is triggered by things we cannot control, like chronic pain or people we are unable to remove from our lives. But the harder it is to accept the things you cannot change, the greater your mastery over negativity will become, and the prouder you can be of your achievements.

As we discussed in Chapter 3, it's important to surrender to the moment by accepting and staying in the present. We cannot change the past, but we can change how we go into the future.

> *"In every day, there are 1,440 minutes. That means we have 1,440 daily opportunities to make a positive impact."*

—**Les Brown, American motivational speaker**

Two: Identify Negativity Triggers

The next thing is to see what flips the negative switch in yourself. (This is a topic we briefly touched on in Chapter 3, when we discussed the "challenge" aspect of the L.U.C.Y circle, an important piece of the positivity pie.)

The average person processes up to 60,000 separate thoughts a day; 90 percent of those are subconscious thoughts.[17] Subconscious thoughts are automatic ones that are produced by our minds on a subconscious level and continue to be produced without any conscious effort or input from our conscious mind. This means we think about things all day and night long without consciously trying to do so. If you were to think of your mind as a minicomputer, these are computer programs that automatically respond to stimuli in our environments.

---

[17] *Power of Positive Thinking,* by Ira Vineyard, Chapter 2. Published by lulu. com, 2016.

Our environment, therefore, plays a key role in our mindset and subconscious thought processes. For example, we may smile and say we are happy, but deep down, we are sad because of a horrible childhood. It is the subconscious mind that stimulates either the positive or negative thought patterns that guide us through our lives. This suggests that if you are subconsciously preprogrammed to be negative, you will function as such. Subconscious negativity stunts our evolution and stops us reaching our goals. These automatic thoughts are called "success blockers." Automatic thoughts prevent you from being successful because they determine your patterns, behaviors, and attitudes.

It has been scientifically observed that "automatic thoughts" are actually triggered by belief patterns called "schema" that are shared by a group of people who share the same challenges and/or limitations in their lives.[18] This means that seeking out a community of people who have been through something similar (a support group for sufferers of a specific disease, for example) might be counterproductive.

So, the battle to regain a positive mindset could be a matter of changing the environment in which you operate. But before you can do that, you must eliminate the thoughts that create the negative mindset in the first place. This is done by determining consciously what things—whether thoughts or patterns—block our positive selves on a day-in-day-out basis. These are our limiting and negative thoughts, attitudes, and

---

[18] Ira Vineyard, *The Power of Positive Thinking: For people who want to learn how changing your thinking can change your world for the better,* (lulu.com, 2016, page 9)

behaviors that we can start to control when we think about them. This is because we see how they manifest in us and then become a part of our daily thoughts and behaviors. If you don't pinpoint the sources of negativity, you cannot change them. It's that simple.

Don't forget the "L.U.C.Y" circle. When you apply those actions, you start to understand how it all comes together and how you can change your negative thoughts, attitudes, and behaviors to more positive ones throughout your day.

The challenge here is honesty. Our triggers can seem either too petty to admit or so deep as to be too painful to confront. But without honesty, we'll continue to let events set us on a familiar negativity spiral that could be avoided if we were aware of its role in our lives as a trigger.

So, come on then, let's lay our cards on the table, and in the spirit of reciprocity, I'll show my hand first. The following is a list of the common things that ignite a spark of negativity in me:

- When someone doesn't pick up something I've taught them as quickly as I think they should.
- People who leave things on their to-do list for too long for no reason I can discern.
- People who hold up the security line at the airport when they had been waiting long enough to prepare for the screening!

Silly stuff, right? But these everyday annoyances can turn your day from a positive one to a negative in a very short amount of time. But it's not as simple as identifying those annoyances.

To uncover the trigger, we need to go one step further and ask ourselves what lies at the root of those triggers.

I'd like to suggest that there are only two roots of our negativity: superiority or inferiority. Perhaps the most dominant is superiority, i.e., the attitude of "my way is better" and judging others by your own standards. Because I don't leave things on my to-do list for too long, I think nobody else should. Or because I travel frequently, the TSA (Transportation Security Administration) rules for security screenings are clear and obvious to me; so how on earth is it possible that other people don't know you're supposed to take your shoes off?! On the other hand, the inferiority root cause is about how others' behavior reflects on us. When I am bothered by someone's inability to grasp what I've taught them, do I fear that I am not a good teacher? It's easier to blame them for their failure than to accept it might somehow be my fault. Perhaps it is the inferiority causes that are the hardest to accept, because there may be some genuine fear or past trauma to deal with.

Activity: Trigger Analysis

So, now it's your turn. Nobody is going to read your list, unless you want them to, so be brutally honest with yourself, starting with four kinds of scenario or types of person. Continue this analysis in a notebook as you continue to recognize your triggers:

Scenario or Type of Person	Negative emotion	Emotional root: superiority or inferiority?

Whether the root is superiority or inferiority, the problem is you! You will almost certainly not be able to change someone's learning style, or their ability to organize their life, or their understanding of the seemingly arbitrary rules of air travel; you can only change yourself.

When you notice the triggers, then you can stop them from making you react negatively and putting you in a negative frame of mind. This is when our L.U.C.Y circle comes in useful. This is easier said than done, but once you start catching yourself as your thoughts become negative, changing them into a positive, it becomes easier. The more aware you are of when you are becoming negative, and changing the negativity as it arises, the more you will notice you are changing things that are negative in your life to positive, as well. Positive thoughts create positive actions and give positive results.

Once the triggers have been identified, the next step in regaining your positive mindset is to consciously and actively change those thoughts you have that keep you blocked and in a negative mindset—a subject we'll return to in the next chapter.

Three: Self-Esteem

I am aware that, so far, I've asked you to look at where you might be falling short. Perhaps by this point in the book, you're even feeling a little dispirited—and if that's the case, let's redress the imbalance by focusing on what you feel good about in your life. Why? Because when we are feeling good about ourselves, everything around us seems brighter. A healthy level of self-confidence and self-esteem is not only necessary, it is essential for any kind of success we seek. Only when you're comfortable with who you are and confident in what you can do, will other people believe in you and your abilities. This applies both to your personal life as well as your professional life.

1. **Recognizing your unique skills, talents, and capabilities**

   This is not only important from a professional or personal development perspective, it also enables you to align your uniqueness in its entirety with your potential. Some studies reveal that we are the happiest and most effective when we can utilize our individual abilities to the highest degree possible. The findings of one UK study suggested that, compared to people who didn't feel they were playing to their strengths in life, people who were using their talents experienced more positive emotions, greater vitality, and improved sense of self-worth.[19]

   But first, we must identify what those abilities are, even if we generally dislike blowing our own horn!

   Take some time to think about it now. And just like admitting to our negativity triggers, remember that nobody needs to see your list!

---

[19] http://www.actionforhappiness.org/take-action/find-your-strengths-and-focus-on-using-them (September 2017). Accessed April 2018.

Activity: Talent Audit

List *anything* you consider yourself good at regarding your professional life and your personal life. Even the seemingly most frivolous things count: maybe you kick butt at karaoke or you keep on top of your personal finances. Whatever you do that makes you feel good about yourself, take the time to recognize them here, or note them in a journal. And whenever you feel low, come back to the list and smile.

And if you're either too low to see your talents, ask a close friend, relative, or colleague to help.

Things I excel at	Things I'm good at

Also, if you did the VIA Survey mentioned in Chapter 4, visit this online resource for a list of key strengths that you might exhibit and can develop: www.psychologytoday.com/blog/what-matters-most/201505/new-ways-happiness-strengths

2. Banish the Trash Talk

In order to live in positivity, we must make sure the conversations we have with ourselves and about ourselves are always positive. If we are negative with our own feelings, how can we be positive with anything (or anyone) else in our lives? Negativity, in essence, is nothing more than resistance to the positive, so once you consciously decide you will live a positive life, then you reinforce the idea into your subconscious with your internal dialogs.

We often tell ourselves negative things, so ridding your thought patterns of certain tendencies is certainly a tough challenge. But the first step to squashing the damaging thought patterns is to recognize them.

Our brains are great at making up rational excuses for inaction, and we're endlessly capable of inventing "good reasons" for why certain things don't get done. While we believe in these good excuses, positive change cannot be initiated. Which of the following are you prone to?

- *"I'm not good enough."*

  One of the key reasons why most people never reach their full potential is rooted in variations on the belief of not being good enough. This isn't something people often say aloud, but it's a constant buzz of self-doubt, and this negative thought tops the chart of major "success blockers."

- *"Better the devil you know than the devil you don't."*

  Resistance to change is rooted in the fear of the unknown. It is often evidenced by people who, despite their unhappiness with their situation, don't fully explore opportunities for change. This resistance often leads to missed opportunities for advancement.

- *"They're counting on me."*

  Perception of dependencies and co-dependencies comes in many forms. The result, however, is mostly the erroneous belief that we are responsible for others' happiness and success (or ours is dependent on others). Cognitive patterns reflecting the necessity to earn the approval or love of other people can create serious limitations on many fronts. We can be supportive and helpful to others while staying true to ourselves.

- *"It's not my fault."*

  We've all blamed others for missed opportunities from time to time, believing that someone had stood in the way of our success. If these experiences turn into core beliefs that we carry with us, consciously or unconsciously, we create not only excuses for not progressing, but also obstacles to recognizing ways to work around them and achieve our goals.

• *"That'll never work."*

Pessimism: the perennial victim! There are multiple root causes of negative expectations, but the one thing they all have in common is their tendency to create self-fulfilling prophecies. If your mind tells you, "I can't possibly do that," chances are these predictions will become a reality. Pessimists often feel life is a constant struggle and the next negative event is just around the corner. Imagine an athlete going into the Olympic Games thinking *I can't possibly win*—they might surprise themselves, but it's more likely they'd destroy their potential.

• *"I don't deserve it."*

This is a variation on the first excuse (I'm not good enough), but rather than it being about your ability, it's about your perception of what's rightfully yours. Perhaps it's born of guilt or some regret, but this attitude of martyrdom will doom you to failure.

• *"It's written in the stars."*

This attitude is the hallmark of the fatalist. Victims of circumstance tend to accept unhappiness, mediocrity, or failure as part of their destiny. What they fail to realize is that they often have the power to change their circumstances. Instead, they simply accept their lot in life with passivity.

- *"I'll do it later."*

  Procrastination be gone! Positive change always requires an orientation toward action. The best objectives and plans don't mean anything if there's no follow-through. Never take "tomorrow" for granted, because one day, it will not come.

3. Affirmations

We have touched on affirmations already in our discussion of the M.O.M.E.N.T. technique, but I want to return to it again because it's so important.

If you suffer from low self-esteem, it isn't enough to banish the trash talk; you must replace it with positive thought patterns. This is where I throw a science word at you: neuroplasticity.

Neuroplasticity refers to your brain's ability to rewire itself. Thought patterns form what's known as "neuro-networks" and these are associated with certain emotions. Hopefully, the neuro-net that stores information about your experience of love, for example, is positive, so that when you think about someone you love, it releases the chemicals in your brain that generate plenty of warm, joyous feelings. On the flip side, the neuro-nets can store very negative information (as we saw in the trash talk section above), and every time a negative trigger occurs, your brain is flooded with chemicals that make you feel bad.

Simply speaking, affirmations work by interrupting the thought patterns held in these neuro-nets. And it's not new science. It was first brought into the public consciousness by French psychologist Emile Coué in the 1920s, and since then many scientists have come to believe that affirmations reset the chemical pathways in the brain. Studies have shown that people perform better in high-stress situations if they practice affirmations. A 2013 research project by Carnegie Mellon University[20] showed that students scored better grade point averages if they practiced affirmations at the start of the school year. You can also see affirmations at work in sports. Many of the sporting greats have a supreme confidence that borders on arrogance ahead of a race or a match, but this is simply the psychological technique of affirmation.

4. Meeting Your Goals

A powerful source of self-esteem is achieving something you set out to achieve, whether it's a daily target or a long-term goal. This is something we'll explore more in Chapter 6.

---

20 Creswell JD, Dutcher JM, Klein WMP, Harris PR, Levine JM, "Self-Affirmation Improves Problem-Solving under Stress," 2013. PLoS ONE 8(5): e62593. doi:10.1371/journal.pone.0062593

"It's the repetition of affirmations that leads to belief. And once that belief becomes a deep conviction, things begin to happen. "

—**Muhammad Ali, American boxer**

Victim to Victor

"We are not a victim of our emotions or thoughts. We can understand our triggers and use them as tools to help us respond more objectively."

—Elizabeth Thornton, romance writer

As a small child at age four, my mom wanted to help her mother make hot cocoa. The kettle was heating on the stove, and my mom wanted to stir the hot cocoa. So, she climbed up on a step stool so that she could reach the stovetop and started to slowly stir the boiling water; what happened next will cause even the toughest people to cringe. Her flannel pajamas caught on fire from the hot stove, and her entire chest was covered with third-degree burns.

My uncles would tell stories about how they would distract their younger sisters when my grandparents had to change the bandages on my mom's burns. The older brothers would escort them out of the house and walk for blocks away to avoid hearing my mom screaming in pain. My aunt recalled this time and told me: "*Dad didn't have a job and Mom was working as a nurse's aide. We didn't have any health insurance, so they [the doctors] allowed Mom and Dad to change Ronda's dressings. I would leave the house because she would scream so loudly. Kind of a dark time in our family.*"

I can't begin to imagine what that must have been like for a four-year-old child. And right after that incident, the family all moved to a different town to care for my mom's grandmother, who was dying of cancer.

Amazingly, my mom didn't take those physical scars and make them mental ones. But that wasn't to be the last challenge my mom would face. She experienced more loss in her life than anyone else I know. She lost her grandmother to pancreatic cancer and, as a teenager, watched her own mother die from the agony of this horrible disease, as well. If that wasn't bad enough, within the last six years of her life, she also lost both of her brothers to this same, horrific disease. She also supported her twin sister through breast cancer and battled her own fight against skin cancer.

Despite all this pain, emotional and physical, she chose not to be a victim of her circumstances, which I find remarkable.

Here is a picture of my mom and her family, the Eatherton siblings. My mom is pictured in the middle row on the left: the one winking, of course! The beautiful woman on the right is my mom's mom, Nadine.

From those pictured below, the only ones that remain is my mom's twin sister, Ranae, pictured in the middle row on the right, and my mom's youngest sister, Tami (front row).

You have a choice, too. Are you going to be a victim? Or are you going to be a victor? If you make a choice to be the victor, you can start connecting with others and be a friend to those you interact with. If you choose to be a victim, you will push people away.

We simply don't want to be around victims. I once had an employee who was incredibly negative, for whom everything that happened to her was the worst thing in the world. Whenever management changed something, she would instantly see the problems with it and resist the change. She drove me crazy! But once I started to get to know her, I started to understand where she was coming from. I didn't agree with it, but it gave me the framework for understanding. You see, she had a rough childhood and felt like she was taken advantage of. As a woman in a male-dominated industry, she felt she had to work ten times harder, and to overcome this sense of victimization, she built a "tough-girl" negative wall as protection. She allowed herself to be a victim of her circumstances and used negativity to separate herself from others.

This chapter is concerned with how you might walk in victory, not victimhood.

Positivity in Adversity

The hardest challenge in positivity is to remain positive when we are faced with adversity. The true test of being positive is the solutions we find to overcome the adversity. Staying positive in troubled times can take a lifetime to learn, but it can be done.

Sometimes during adversity, we feel "broken." It's okay to be broken; it's how we put ourselves back together that reveals everything. Getting back to "normal" is important. But what is "normal"? Sometimes you must reestablish what normal is. I remember my dad telling me this one late evening as we were sitting at the kitchen island, both exhausted from being at the hospital all day. He said, "Amy, as we know it, normal will never be normal again. Your mom will never be able to come home. We need to reestablish what 'normal' is." Profound. And he was right. Normal would no longer be having family dinners at the kitchen table. Normal would never be my mom waking up in her own bed. Normal would never be happy hour on my parents' back deck, laughing and enjoying a few beers. Our "new normal" meant daily visits to the hospital. Instead of family dinners at the kitchen table, it would mean feeding my mom because she could no longer feed herself. It meant grabbing hospital food from the cafeteria if we had a couple of minutes to spare. Our new normal was the daily drive to the hospital instead of daily happy hours on the porch. And instead of laughs, maybe a few more tears. Once you can define your new normal, then you can accept it and ultimately overcome it.

The main thing is that when you are facing a problem, you get to the source of what is making the negativity and try to put an end to it, so you can endure on. Negative factors can really take a toll on everything you do. It sets in your mind that you cannot succeed or overcome your problems. Negativity instills in us that there is no solution to a bad situation, so we just have to wallow in it and accept it. If you have trouble staying positive during a difficult time, then it is suggested you write the problem down and research ways to alleviate the problem. You may come to find others, when you research, who have the same problems you do, and that you are not alone.

Being positive is one of the best traits a person can have. It keeps you proactive to succeed in your life despite the odds against you. It activates your inner strength and allows you to remain in control of even the worst situations. Staying positive in hard times is also a sign of maturity. It takes a mature person to stay positive when bombarded by negativity and problems.

Here are some tips to use to stay positive under adverse conditions:

Inspiration. When the going gets tough, find other people who have gone through what you are going through and have risen above it. You can use their story to keep you inspired to not give up and to remain positive, as they did.

Influences. Friends and family can be a source of both comfort and support when you are going through rough times. If someone doesn't give you positive reinforcement in times of trouble, then leave him or her alone. You don't need anyone or anything to tear you down when you are fighting for your life to be better. Also surround yourself with goal-driven people whom you admire.

Diversion. Avoid wallowing for too long or sidestep negativity by doing something fun and absorbing. Take a class and do that thing you never got around to doing. Read or meditate. Do whatever you need to keep yourself up in a positive frame of mind. If overdone, this can turn into running away from your problems, so try to ensure your diversions are there for reprieve from your troubles.

Persistence. By not giving up, even under the hardest conditions, you find, deep within, that tiny bit of strength inside, even if you thought it was all gone.

Relaxation. Tension breeds negativity and adversity. Try to meditate, listen to music, practice yoga, get a massage, pamper yourself within your means, take a warm bath … whatever it takes. And keep reminding yourself that there is light at the end of the tunnel.

Gratitude. You may not have a lot materially, but you will have a surprising number of things to be grateful for in your life, if you can take a few minutes at the beginning and end of your day to recognize them.

Exercise. It will release endorphins into your body and you WILL feel better. Exercise has been proven to be key in the treatment of depression.

Love. Tell someone you love them! By giving out love spontaneously, you will get it back in unexpected ways.

Law of Attraction—but Not without Action!

I'm sure you've heard the phrase "Law of Attraction" before. It is a favorite term of the life-coaching community, and plenty has been written about it in depth elsewhere (which you can discover for yourself).

Despite its modern popularity, the idea of attraction was first taught by Buddha, or so the story goes. In 391 BC, Plato built on the ideas of the Greek philosophers who went before him about phila (attractive force) and neikos (repulsive force). He illustrated the "like attracts like" theory using examples of water-to-water and earth-to-earth. As humans, we are attracted to water because 60 percent of our bodies comprises water (so it's perhaps no coincidence that 80 percent of the world's population lives within 60 miles of the coast). Later, in 1250 AD, Albertus Magnus expanded this idea and applied affinity to chemical systems and postulated the law of affinity.[21]

---

[21] https://www.tokenrock.com/explain-law-of-attraction-28.html, accessed
April 2018.

This sounds very complicated, but in fact, the law is simple: Put good things out into the universe, and good things will come back. *It's karma. It's what goes around comes around.*

Thoughts are a creative process, and like any craft, it is possible to learn new skills. The mind is fertile ground and thoughts are seeds. If you plant a seed and nurture it, it grows. If you nurture it with positive water, you get a positive plant. If you water it with negativity, a negative plant will grow. Thoughts manifest by the attention we give them, be it good or bad. So, to manifest positive thoughts, we must give them the positive attention they need to flourish.

I call the creation of positive thought "focused daydreaming." When you daydream with focus, you put yourself in best-case scenario and imagine getting that positive thing you want. It sets the tone in our subconscious to program us to obtain what we want. As a picture I had on the wall in my old home said, "Daydream until your dreams come true." This is how some people who, seemingly against all odds, accomplish something others said was impossible. The more things one adds to the focused daydream such as colors, sounds, scents, and feelings, the more real it becomes.

Why does this work? The subconscious doesn't differentiate between reality and imagination. Everything is real in our subconscious, and our subconscious helps turn thought to reality. The more you visualize positivity and you together in the scene, the more it begins to manifest in your life. In this regard, it comes to light and becomes reality in a natural way. It's like putting new software in a computer, and as you use it, you see more and more of its benefits. The process of practical daydreaming can be used for changing or improving any habit, ability, or skill. You can use it to change your circumstances, and people who are successful use it all the time.

To some people, it might sound like metaphysical woo-woo, especially if those people are facing some of life's toughest challenges, such as unemployment, homelessness, and illness. It's not easy to put out good vibes in these circumstances, but it can actually help to get you out of your situation. When one is worried, fearful, and stressed, it is far harder to think clearly about solutions.

The law of attraction says we bring things into manifestation based on our thoughts and beliefs. And it's this oversimplification of the law of attraction that leads its critics to scoff at it. They say you cannot summon a ten-bedroom mansion just by believing you will one day own it! The law is ineffective without action or intent.

The way I think of the law of attraction is that it must begin as a thought or desire before any action can be taken. Here is an example: Let's say you never finished college, and one morning, the idea about going back comes into your head. The thought may stay with you for a while—a few days, weeks, months, or even a year, but it's in your head. Once that idea in your head keeps popping up, you start to examine the possibilities and find it is a doable possibility. So, now the thought is becoming a belief that you can act on to make happen. Once the thought is backed up by the belief, it's up to you to take the next step. In this case, it would be to take the proper steps to go back to the college.

The law of attraction is a thought that turns into a belief that turns into an action. It operates in three stages:

1. Thought
2. Belief
3. Follow-through

You can have fun with vision boards (a board that includes visual images that represent what you want to achieve in life) all you like, but unless you're acting upon the thought and the belief, nothing will happen (but you will have a pretty collage, covered in lovely images and glitter to hang on your wall).

We'll talk more about the action part of this a little later in this chapter, but for now, I want you to start with step one. Think good thoughts, and the rest will flow from there.

Simply begin by thinking about your day. What happened that was good? It doesn't matter how small that incident was; it may just be that you met someone who could become a friend, or perhaps the weather was simply perfect. Got something?

Now we take it a step further and celebrate it! If you thought of something big, that celebration might be a full throated WOOHOO! Or if it was a small thing, you might just smile about it. Sounds silly? Well, think again. You see, when you do this, when you constantly find things to celebrate, your brain produces "happy" chemicals. By remembering the positive events of your day, your brain will replicate the release of the happy chemicals that were released in the original moment itself: a double hit! The more of these chemicals your brain produces, the more it craves. It wants that same feeling again and again and again; it's almost like an addiction. That's how you live a more positive, happy life, and it all starts with your mindset. My mom was a master at this; she celebrated life, no matter how small the victories!

The positivity mindset you are working toward consists of these elements:

1. Looking at the brighter side of a situation and choosing to stay optimistic
2. Finding reasons to smile more often
3. Having faith in yourself and the universe
4. Associating yourself with happy people
5. Challenging yourself to try new things
6. Watching, reading, or listening to inspirational stories
7. Learning to manage your emotions
8. Developing your meditation practice

If you can instill these things in your life, you are on the way to attracting positive things to you, because you'll give off the same positivity. You will become a positivity magnet and a negativity repellant.

Points 1 to 4 above are about attitudinal changes, which are entirely within your power to make. However, points 6, 7, and 8 are things that have a more practical aspect to them, so I'd like to address these specifically.

Listening for Inspiration: The Speech of Angels

I like to find inspiration in music. For me, music is an expression of emotions. I grew up in a house where music was always playing on the speakers in the house. In my younger years, I started by listening to records, then CDs, and now digital. My monthly subscription to Spotify is a bill I am always willing to pay. Every year in January, I make a new playlist for that year. A playlist that I will listen to time and time again—songs that speak to me at that time in my life and provide me the inspiration I need to accomplish my big goals that year. Every year has a new theme, depending on what my goal is for that year. Now, when I go back and listen to playlists of past years, it brings back memories of all the good things I was able to achieve during that year.

My friend Kevin, music lover and aficionado, often refers to music as the speech of angels. My mom coped with her final days through music. She loved music. Everyone knew that before you left her hospice room at night, you had to be sure to turn on her tablet, which would play her favorite country music station, or perhaps some traditional oldies. Even in the absence of words, music seemed to carry on the conversation. I still have a playlist on my Spotify titled "Lucy's Favorites." In the end, when my mom's communication abilities were limited, she was able to speak to us through music. I would simply ask her, sitting next to her hospice bed, "What song do you want to listen to?" Her answer always revealed the truth—how she was feeling in that moment. Some of her most requested songs were "Hey Jude" by the Beatles, a request for "Honey" by Bobby Goldsboro would mean she was thinking of her mom, and "Time in a Bottle" by Jim Croce meant she was feeling especially sad. I remember one time when I played that song for her, tears rolling down her cheeks, her head tilted to one side as she looked up at me, squeezing my hand. No words were needed. The lyrics spoke her truth. I encourage you to listen to "Time in a Bottle" and take a moment to really hear the lyrics and their meaning. See if those words speak to you as much as they did to my mom and me on that day.

Just as the song "Honey" reminded my mom of her mom, I also have songs that remind me of mine. These hits include "Pretty Woman" by Roy Orbison, "Suspicious Minds" by Elvis Presley, and "But for the Grace of God" by Keith Urban. Perhaps my favorite reminder is "Amarillo by Morning" by George Strait—a country classic that my friend Kevin's dad and local music celebrity, Kelly, sang to my mom while she was in hospice. My mom sitting there in her wheelchair, Kelly sitting next to her with his guitar on his knee beautifully singing one of her favorites! I watched my mom sing along with Kelly, but instead of seeing a woman slouched in her wheelchair savoring what time she had left, I saw the energetic, spunky woman who, just years prior, was "whoop-whooping" in excitement after purchasing tickets to a country music festival at the Texas Cowboys stadium. Her date for the festival? Me! I was twenty years old at the time, and just starting to appreciate country music. My mom was most excited about the headliner for the festival, George Strait.

Now every time I hear that song, I think of this day. This picture is of my mom and me that day, holding our tickets, just before leaving for the show.

After Kelly's visit that day, it warmed my heart to learn that I wasn't the only one thinking of that memory; so was my mom. As she revealed to me that this picture was her "favorite picture of us," I knew we must have been thinking  the same thing at the same time. Perhaps Kevin is right: perhaps music really is the speech of angels.

Activity: Feel the Groove

Just as my mom had difficulty communicating her thoughts and feelings in the end, sometimes we find it challenging to put into words our emotions around any given situation. This is when we can turn to music. Here is an exercise that will help you through expressing your thoughts and feelings.

Think of a situation you currently are facing. Now, find three songs that describe how you are feeling toward that situation.

Song Title	How does this song make you feel?	What part of the song speaks most to you and why?

Managing Negative Emotions

1. Change the channel

What does your Netflix homepage keep recommending you watch? Does it match you with dark, sulking thrillers? Angry documentaries about global injustice? Netflix is great at picking up on patterns and then perpetuating them, just like your mind! You have to deliberately choose something "out of character" to avoid being stuck in a rut on Netflix, and the same applies to your thoughts.

Changing the negative mindset patterns is called cognitive modification. We change how we think from the subconscious level up by reconditioning the old thought patterns we have and replacing them with new ones. If we use the computer analogy, again, we are replacing an old worn out program with a new, better one that functions at optimum speed.

2. Express feelings appropriately

Hanging on to the feelings that are causing you stress, anxiety, or sadness can make you feel worse, both emotionally and physically. You already know this, I'm sure. It is okay to tell someone that there is something bothering you. The main thing is you get the help and support you need to become positive in your life for you.

Of course, I am not suggesting that you not have feelings, or never allow yourself to feel sad. I remember standing amongst the crowd of people, all dressed in black. I was toward the back of the group standing on my tiptoes trying to get a glimpse of my uncle Terry's casket and trying to keep my heels from sinking into the soft ground at the cemetery. I couldn't stop staring at my grandpa as he sat in a chair next to his own son's casket. He was crying. I realized how incredibly sad it was that he had lost a wife and two children in his lifetime. At that point in time, I never would have believed that he would later have to bury yet one more child, my mom. I slowly turned my attention from grandpa to my mom; she looked stoic as if she were numb to tragedy. I don't know what she was thinking as her brother's casket was being lowered into the ground, but later in life randomly, she would get "weepy" and say, "I sure do miss my brothers."

I suppose emotion comes in waves and shouldn't be judged. I know for me, I can be "strong" most of the time when talking about my mom, but sometimes it will just hit me and come out of nowhere. This seems to happen when I am alone—just me and my thoughts. Most of the time while 30,000 feet in the air on a plane to my next speaking engagement, I will find my thoughts overtaken by "I sure do miss my mom." With tears rolling down my cheeks, I peer out the small airplane window in hopes the person next to me doesn't notice.

Perhaps one of the most useful ways to express yourself is in writing. Simply unburdening yourself onto the page is amazingly therapeutic. When I would catch myself in the sky thinking of my mom, that's when I would pull out my computer and write the stories you are reading in this book.

It's important to address negative feelings but to also keep track of the positive ones. If you have to write them down to keep track of them, then do so. Keeping a positivity journal to look at when you feel negative is very helpful. Write in it all the things that make you feel both happy and peaceful so when you need to be reminded you can read them.

Research has shown that writing out life experiences, especially major events (both good and bad), is great for our well-being. Writing about negative experiences helps us process traumatic events, but it's interesting that writing about positive events is also highly beneficial. One study asked subjects to write about an "intensely positive experience" (IPE) or a "neutral topic." The researchers measured the mood of the participants both before and after the writing exercise and revealed that writing about IPEs correlated with positive moods and fewer health center visits.[22] So, don't limit your journaling to the bad days!

A positive outlook gives way to a better quality of life as well as a health boost. People live longer when they are in a positive mindset. Being positive may also mean that you will need to let go of those things that overwhelm and stress you out in your life. It's also important to make time for those things you enjoy.

3. Life balance

At the Positive Life Company, we don't talk about work-life balance anymore; for us, it's just about "life balance." And why is that? Well, work and life are interdependent. As much as we might want to, we don't leave our personal life at home when we sit down at our desk each day. Also, shouldn't employees be excited to get to work? Shouldn't they be so excited that they don't leave their jobs when they go home for the weekend? If an employee loves their job, the job will come home with them, and that is fine with them (and their family). Finally, our coworkers are our second family, and our company is a kind of parent. We look after each other and we expect to be taken care of. So, when you spend two-thirds of your life at work, you should choose something that is going to make you happy!

---

[22] Burton, C. M., & King, L. A. (2004). "The health benefits of writing about intensely positive experiences." Journal of Research in Personality, 38, 150-163.

At home or at work, try not to obsess about those things that cause the negative feelings in the first place. This does not mean to pretend to be happy when you are not; what it means is to deal with the source of the negative feelings, so they are not overwhelming your sense of self and positivity in your life.

4. Calm your body and mind

When our emotions and bodies are in harmony, we tend to be positive. It's important to do things to maintain the body and mind's state of balance. Relaxation techniques such as meditation or guided thoughts help in this regard.

Meditation

Exercise like Yoga, Tai Chi, or simply walking is good for your mind and body. My mom would walk every day on her lunch breaks. Whether there was snow on the ground or sun in the sky, she rarely missed a day. This was one of the signs when we knew something wasn't right with my mom. Naps in her car replaced lunch-break walks. This was the tumor affecting her exhaustion. She had really enjoyed this activity. Walking has been found to reduce psychological stress and improve quality of life.[23] I believe this was one of my mom's secrets to her overall positive attitude in life.

---

[23] Teut, M., Roesner, E. J., Ortiz, M. et al., (2013). "Mindful Walking in Psychologically Distressed Individuals: A Randomized Controlled Trial." *Evidence-Based Complementary and Alternative Medicine*, Volume 2013 (2013), Article ID 489856, http://dx.doi.org/10.1155/2013/489856

You may be thinking to yourself, "That's great, Amy, but I don't have an hour a day to walk!" Well, with anything, it takes commitment (more on that in Chapter 9), but the great thing about walking is you do it all day—you just don't think about it. So, what if you capitalized on all your walks you take during the day? Just think about how many walking moments you experience in one day—walking to your car, walking into the grocery store, walking into your office, etc. Take those walking moments and start to incorporate mindfulness with these short trips. Next time you are walking, think about how your body moves, how your feet feel on the ground, the muscles you are engaging. This helps you to become aware and present in the moment. Mindfulness walking doesn't take any extra time during the day, and it has the same goal as meditation.

BONUS

Go to http://thepositivelifeco.com/seven-more-days for an audio exercise you can download for your next mindful-walking experience.

Whatever it takes for you, in this regard, to help you calm and keep balanced is positive. Stretching and deep breathing are also good. There are plenty of other books out there that will give you some great meditation techniques, so I won't belabor the issue here. However, I will tell you that I personally love hypnosis. We aren't talking about the kind you see on TV or on stage. Hypnosis is, in fact, a highly effective meditation technique to deal with all sorts of issues such as anxiety, low self-esteem, smoking cessation, and so on. In particular, I recommend the app called "Sleep Well" by Insomnia and Sleeping Sounds, which is great for getting a good night's sleep and waking refreshed and ready to face the day with positivity. There will be other apps for other issues, too, so explore what's available online.

When you are ready to take your "Mute" practice from M.O.M.E.N.T. to the next level, try meditating.

Joel Pilka, my cofounder of the Positive Life Company, says that meditation has been key to his success, and he practices it every day. It has helped calm his thoughts, dissolve negativity, lower his heart rate, and reduce stress.

It didn't come naturally to him at first; he says it is a process. But over the years, he has found that three things are critical to making your chosen meditation technique effective:

1. **Consistency.** You have to TRY to do it every day, or at least on a regular basis. It can be different and uncomfortable for people who have never done it, but trying on a consistent basis is half the battle.

2. **No judgment.** Try to just let your brain go where it wants to go. Do not make any judgment. Your brain will decide what it needs at that moment. Embrace it. It may be energizing or calming, but whatever it is, it is okay.

3. **Start small.** Try meditating for just five minutes per day at first. Then, working your way up to twenty minutes. No matter how much time you accomplish, celebrate that, and by starting small, you will be able to build on your success.

Activity: Creative Visualization Meditation

Creative visualization is not a quick magical fix. It's an approach to changing a state of mind and being. Sometimes you may see quick results, and at other times, it takes work and is a longer process. That is how life is. With creative visualization, we dream realistic dreams and change them to what we want to be better in our lives. For instance, if you live in a little cramped apartment, why not dream for a bigger home? Change your thoughts; see yourself in that bigger apartment or home and feel yourself living in it. Visualize and believe that you are living in a bigger apartment. This helps overcome our limited thinking. It is limited thinking that keeps us from getting what we want in life. The more open-minded we are, the more possibilities to manifest what we want there are.

Here are some guidelines to use in approaching creative visualization:

---

1. Sit alone in a quiet place where you will not be disturbed.

2. Get comfortable and relax your body by tensing and releasing each muscle one by one (don't forget your face—we carry a lot of tension there!).

3. Determine the desire or outcome you want to achieve. This should be something you can picture, i.e., something real (e.g., a bigger apartment), not abstract (e.g., happiness).

4. Believe that goodness will result from your visualization, for you and for others.

5. Breathe rhythmically and deeply several times.

6. Visualize a clear and detailed mental image of the thing you desire or want to accomplish.

7. Use all senses in your visualization: sight, sound, touch, smell and taste.

8. Attach positive feelings to your mental image (joy, love, pride, peace, satisfaction, hope, etc.)

9. Meditate on that image for a full ten minutes.

I recommend visualizing and meditating once a day. Persevere with your visualization day after day, with patience, hope, and belief.

Now that you've banished the victim and welcomed the victor into your life, the next critical step is to lay the foundations of your victory—with a plan!

Stop Wanting, Start Doing!

I hear it all the time: "I want to be happier. I want to be more positive. I want to be more fulfilled." Well, what are you waiting for?

The good news is that the visualization technique discussed above will train your conscious mind to become aware of its subconscious desires. This meditation practice makes you more aware of opportunities that pop up, and lets the subconscious mind motivate you to take action, instead of just waiting for things to happen.

However, visualization alone cannot take you where you want to go. For one thing, practicing visualization will be less effective if you have not defined the big-picture goals for your life.

The main purpose for incorporating positivity in our lives is to achieve our dreams and goals. There are several factors you need to consider if you are to make your dreams a reality. The success of achieving what you want depends overall on the following things:

1. You should have a specific goal.
2. You must be sure you really want to achieve your goal.
3. You need to have a clear mental image of your goal.

4. You need a strong desire.

5. You need to disregard and reject doubts and thoughts about failure.

6. You need confidence and faith so that you can persevere until you gain success.

The things above sound simple enough, but few people really apply them toward getting what they want. Don't be one of those people.

So, what is your goal?

People make mistakes when they think that big goals mean only things like being wealthy, having an expensive car, having a big house with a pool, or building a business empire. These are big goals, sure, but a big goal can also be simple, like spending time with loved ones, finding true love, or becoming healthier.

Fixed Mindset vs. Growth Mindset

Carol Dweck first coined the terms "fixed mindset" and "growth mindset."[24] A person with a fixed mindset believes that human qualities cannot be changed in a purposeful way. Examples of a fixed mindset would be thoughts such as: "I'm not good enough." or "I am not smart enough." or "I can't achieve that." A person with a growth mindset believes that human qualities can be improved. A growth mindset would sound like: "I may

---

[24] Carol S. Dweck Ph.D., *Mindset: The New Psychology of Success*, (New York: Random House, 2016)

not have the knowledge to complete this task right now, but I can learn." Having a growth mindset will lead to more success in achieving your goals because you believe you can make a change for the better. Conversely, having a fixed mindset will lead to a standstill because you will not believe that the goal is achievable.

Remember when we discussed neuroplasticity? Your brain is malleable and can change. This is believing in a growth mindset. To shift from a fixed mindset to a growth mindset, you have to first recognize when you have a fixed mindset. Here is an exercise you can complete to shift your mindset from a fixed mindset to a growth mindset so that you can achieve anything you want to achieve.

Fixed Mindset Thought	Change to a Growth Mindset Thought	Action Leading to New Growth Mindset	Celebration Once Growth Mindset Action Is Achieved
Ex: I am not good enough to get my dream job.	I will seek the knowledge needed so that I am a premier candidate for my dream job.	Identify the top 5 skills needed for my dream job and get certified in the skills I do not already possess.	Print certificate of each skill I master and hang on my wall as a reminder of my accomplishment.

Changing your mindset is not an easy feat. It took my mom years to understand this. Even when she knew she was dying, she maintained a growth mindset throughout her therapy. After the tumor was removed and she woke up from her coma, my mom had to learn how to walk again and complete normal daily functions that you and I take for granted. One of my favorite things to do when my mom was in the hospital was visit her during her physical and occupational therapy times. On one particularly sunny day, her therapists decided to have Ronda enjoy the warmth of the sun and complete her therapy outside. The activity was simply to stand up and toss a ring in a bucket about three feet away—a task that was extremely difficult for my mom at the time—just standing up with assistance was a win in itself. There she was on the front lawn of the hospital with Mike and Rachel (her therapists) on either side of her, holding her up so she would not fall to the ground. While helping her to stand, Rachel handed her a red ring and said, "Okay, Ronda, toss it into the bucket!"

"Let's do it!" my mom exclaimed!

At that moment in time, my mom had a growth mindset ("I can do this!"). As she took the red ring from Rachel, she tossed it, but it only went a few inches from her feet. Failure. Now, my mom had a choice to make. She could choose fixed mindset: "This is too hard. I can't do it." Or, she could choose growth mindset: "That was really difficult for me, but I'll try again. This time put more strength in my toss." Determined, she chose the growth mindset, a quality that her therapists cherished about her.

She grabbed the next ring, a pink one this time, grasped it, straightened her arm, pulled it back, swung her arm forward, and released! "Clunk!" The ring landed in the bucket! SUCCESS! She fist-pumped her hand in excitement, and in that moment, that was all the celebration that was needed. Her fist-pump meant everything as I watched from a distance!

> **"** *If you believe in yourself and have dedication and pride—and never quit, you'll be a winner. The price of victory is high but so are the rewards.* **"**

—**Paul Bryant, American Football coach**

Part Three:

Connections
& Community

"What is your favorite childhood memory?" I remember asking my mom while sitting next to her hospice bed, desperate to learn everything I could possibly learn from her. "Going to the stock car races," she said.

My mom's dad and oldest brother were race car drivers, and it seemed that their weekends were consumed by being at the track to cheer them on.

"What about the races did you like?" I asked.

"I liked walking in front of all of the people!"

"Why? Because you wanted to see everyone, or because you wanted everyone to see you?"

"I wanted them to see me. Isn't that weird?" she said.

Now, for the introverted person that my mom seemed to be, it honestly did seem strange. But when you understand that my mom never had an ego, you will realize that what she wanted is what we all want from life—to have connections with others.

You see, she didn't want people to see her so that she could feel popular. Instead, she wanted others to see her so that she felt she existed. That people felt connected to her.

My mom's favorite childhood memory became a reality during her death. Except it wasn't at a racetrack—it was in hospital. She had over 1000 visits from friends and family in eight months. She didn't have to "walk in front of all of the people" because "all of the people" came to her. This is the impact of the connections that my mom made throughout her life.

Aligning the Three Cs

Our ability to contribute to our community will be a lot harder if we have not done the work on our character first. You must be closer to the destination of happiness with yourself before you can connect with others in meaningful ways, and only when we have a good network of connections, can we benefit our community effectively. For example, if you are engaging with your community and you're doing good in the world, but you aren't achieving personal fulfillment, then you're never really going to achieve true happiness.

Think of it like a target divided equally into three sections: Character, Connections, Community. Where is your dart in each of these sections? The closer to the center your darts are, the closer to happiness you are. When you hit the bullseye, you are living life the exactly the way you want to be living.

True happiness comes when you can achieve positivity and happiness at all levels: character, connections, and community.

I recommend doing them in sequential order. For example, you have to achieve positivity and happiness with yourself first (character). However, that's not saying that you can't work on your community at the same time that you're working on your character; they're not independent of one another. All three of your darts must come together toward the center of your target. Once you've mastered your character, developed your connections, and engaged meaningfully at the community level, then they all are aligned and they all come together, and that's when you can achieve true happiness. BULLSEYE!

HAPPINESS TARGET

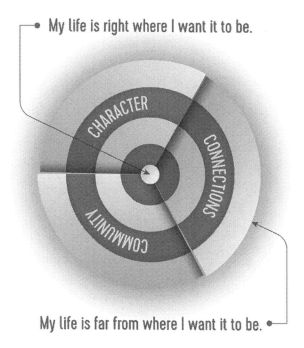

My life is right where I want it to be.

My life is far from where I want it to be.

In this section we'll be looking at the various layers of interactions we all have with others and the impact those connections have on our ability to be happy and positive:

1. Family relations and friendships
2. Community participation
3. Global citizenship

Chapter 7

Inner Circle

> **"***It took me a really long time to decide who I want my circle to be and who I want to surround myself with. Once you make that choice, that is where I feel like I have built my strength. This is my life choice. These are the people that make me feel good about me, and hat I love and adore and will do anything for.* **"**

—Katie Aselton, film director

Who do you turn to when the going gets rough? Your sister or brother? Mom or Dad? Or do you turn to your oldest friend? When our reserve of positivity runs low, we seek out confidants to help pull us through. Those same people are also those with whom we want to share in our happiest moments, too.

Family are important, of course, but sometimes it can be harder to have positive relationships with family members. Indeed, 2017 research published in the journal *Personal Relationships* shows that, as we age, the friendships we have are more important to us than family in terms of our happiness and mental health. The researcher, William Chopik, said: "A few studies show that we often enjoy our time with friends more than with family." He also says, "We do leisurely things with friends, whereas family events are often serious or maybe a little monotonous."[25] It can be a hard thing for families to accept that they don't automatically get the kind of access to your emotions and experiences that your friends do!

For me, it was possible to see my mom as a friend, but it was a choice and it was a process that took several years. When I was growing up, my mom wanted a friendship with me, but I just wanted a mom. I never told her anything that was going on in my life, besides what she had to know, and when I did tell her something, I would downplay everything. As a result, we had a couple of rough years when I was a teenager (I was pretty bratty!), but it was what I considered to be a normal mother-daughter relationship. That began to change when I went to college, as it does for many teenagers, I imagine. The distance between college and home was enough to help me see her not only as a mom but also as more of a person. I would come home from college, and she would just be so excited to see me. We started then to hang out, and I got to see another side of her—she invited me into her inner circle, and I was finally

---

[25] http://time.com/4809325/friends-friendship-health-family/, June 7, 2017 (accessed April 2018)

ready to accept. Gradually, she went from Mom to person. This was illustrated during my speech at the Seniors' Parents' Banquet for my Sorority. During that banquet, my speech to my parents, specifically the part to my mom read:

> Mom, growing up, I never appreciated the gift of a mother, while you understood it more than anyone else. I took you and our relationship for granted. Because you lost your mother at eighteen, you understood, all too well, how important a mother/daughter relationship truly is. Now I understand why you gave 110 percent to me all the time. There were times I know you were frustrated and that all you wanted was to be successful at that "perfect" relationship with me. Mom, you were successful, and I truly do think the world of you. I only hope that I can have your spunky attitude and your tremendous outlook on life when I am your age.

And then, finally, she transitioned from person to friend after college, when I felt ready to invite her into my inner circle. If I were to pinpoint when our friendship really started, it would be when I worked for an electric distributor and lived in Denver, Colorado. I was in mountain time, and they were in central time, so I would call her as I was driving home from work, invariably stuck in commuter traffic, at 5:30 her time, just as she was getting home from work. She would crack a beer and sit on the porch while we talked for an hour. That one thing transformed our relationship. Both of us began to really look forward to that weekly call. When I moved between cities again, that ritual remained, and we talked through FaceTime, with cocktails in hand, at the same time each Friday. And then

I moved to Florida, and the same thing. The point of this story is that friendships take time to develop and to nurture, and they need both parties to be engaged. But when that connection happens, it's magical and meaningful to both of you in ways that will be very important, especially when times get tough. One of the last text messages I ever received from my mom, just five days before she would be admitted for brain tumor said, "Can't wait to Skype tonight!!!!" Which I replied with, "YES!!!!"

Perhaps one of the strongest stories of friendship is how my closest friends showed up during my mom's last days. Interestingly, several of those friends, she considered her "favorites." She always loved my brother's and my friends as if they were her own sons and daughters, and they loved her. Three of her favorites—Nick, Kevin, and Lukas—ended up being honorary pallbearers at her funeral. She chose them for the role as a part of her dying wish.

I guess you don't really understand the power of friendship until you need it most. My friend Tammi said it best, "Friendship is a convenience during good times and a necessity during hard times." I remember telling one of my best friends, Lukas Fenton, in the parking lot of Bryan West Hospital during my first visit home that "In the end, I may not remember everything about this whole journey we are about to embark on, but I will always remember those who were there for me." This statement holds true as I look back.

No doubt, Lukas was my rock, along with Kevin, Nick, Abby, Jamie S., Jenne, and Jamie H., and so many more! It's so incredible to see everyone's best qualities shine through in these rough times.

My friends got me through. Whether it was multiple hospital visits from Lukas, hanging out at my parents' house with Kevin after a long day at the hospital, or Jamie bringing me a coat when I came back to snow on the ground (this beach girl doesn't own a winter jacket). Nick never hesitated to take my phone call, and Abby was always there to simply take a walk with me to get me out of the hospital. Countless other friends supported me during that time in countless different ways, and so it will always be true to me that friendship is never to be taken for granted. Those who came through for me will hold a special place in my heart forever.

Social Capital

Your social circle is one you should spend time on. Our connection to other people—our so-called social capital—is essential to our positivity. But more significantly, humankind has evolved into being a social animal because we understand that community is essential to our survival. This is illustrated using the bear in the woods analogy: If we are alone when we encounter a bear, our chance of survival is minimal; if there are two of us, our chance is greater; but if there are three or more, the bear's chances begin to look very slim indeed. The more people we surround ourselves with, the better our odds of beating that bear! And this sense of protection we get from others is key to happiness.

It is no coincidence that the World Happiness Report uses "social support" as one of its measures. We know instinctively that the more friends we have, the happier we are, and by extension, this makes us more positive about surviving a tough moment. But how many friends should we have? What is the optimum number of people we need for a successful support network?

An evolutionary psychologist called Dr. Robin Dunbar claimed that the human brain could not maintain a connection with more than 150 people, and your closest fifteen people have the most impact on your mental and physical health.[26] This inner circle of fifteen might include family members, but Dunbar believes that friends are better for you because you choose their company (which suggests they are people who make you happy). That happiness your friends create releases endorphins that actually boost your immune system—and we know that healthy people are happier and more positive! I consider myself one of the lucky ones as we have an incredible family that I would choose to be on that short list.

Personal contact is key, though. Your contacts only have value if they are people you see and spend time with *in person*. Unfortunately, your 2,000 friends on Facebook do not count; in fact, they may even be counterproductive. A study in 2014, published in *Computers in Human Behavior*, revealed that only 9 percent of Facebook users' activity involved communicating directly with others.[27]

So, you may be rich in friendships in cyberspace, but take the time now to examine how rich you are in real life connections. And, if you find yourself lacking in this area, you know what to do.

---

[26] https://www.theguardian.com/technology/2010/mar/14/my-bright-idea-robin-dunbar, March 13, 2010 (accessed April 2018)

[27] *Computers in Human Behavior*, Editor: Matthieu Guitton, Volume 84, July 2018

Activity: Fifteen Fantastic Friends

This is an activity designed to identify your inner social circle. If you find it hard to complete the list, you know you should work on making deeper connections. On the other hand, if it's hard to narrow it down to fifteen, consider yourself well connected!

If you were planning a fun weekend away, which seven people of your fifteen would you invite, and why?

1 _____ because _____
_____
_____

2 _____ because _____
_____
_____

3 _____ because _____
_____
_____

4 _____ because _____
_____
_____

5 _____ because _____
_____
_____

6 _____ because _____

_____

7 _____ because _____

_____

If you were in hospital after a serious operation, which seven people from your fifteen would you hope would come to visit you, and why?

1 _____ because _____

_____

2 _____ because _____

_____

3 _____ because _____

_____

4 _____ because _____

_____

5 _____ because _____

_____

```
┌─────────────────────────────────────────────────────────┐
│                                                           │
│   6   _____   because _____  │
│       _____    │
│       _____    │
│   7   _____   because _____  │
│       _____    │
│       _____    │
│                                                           │
└─────────────────────────────────────────────────────────┘
```

Clearing Out Your Inner Circle

This is where I tell you that there may be some seriously negative influences who find themselves, by default, inside your precious inner circle of loved ones. It's inevitable that, at some point, someone you consider a member of your trusted inner circle will let you down. Getting over such an incident can be tough, and you might be tempted to exile that person from your circle. These breaches of trust can eat away at us, and the closer that person is to us, the harder we take the disappointment. If you're the type to cut someone off the moment they transgress, you'll find yourself with a pretty lonely circle of one! It's important to accept that sometimes our loved ones get things wrong—indeed, you have probably been wrong on occasion, too!

When this situation occurs, it can be useful to think about *intention*, rather than impact. You know how you feel because of your friend or family member's actions, but was that what he or she intended?

Positive & Negative Intention

I don't believe in right or wrong; I believe in positive and negative intention. When you see and think in terms of positive or negative intention, your view of people changes. This is one step closer to living a more positive life.

Unless you're dealing with a bona fide psychopath, people rarely mean you any harm. And when you realize this, it changes your mindset. There is no need to direct your negative energy toward that person because they didn't have a negative intention in making you upset. Therefore, technically, they didn't do anything wrong.

Let me illustrate this point by applying it to an encounter with a total stranger. If you are driving and somebody cuts you off, you can get mad and shout at their stupidity or thoughtlessness. Or, you can ask yourself, "Did that person intend to cut me off?" In all probability, that driver didn't see you, because the alternative is that he or she picked out your car of all of the other cars on the road and said, "I can't wait to make this person so mad that it ruins their entire day." That's very unlikely, right? Maybe he had somewhere urgent to be. Maybe he was trying to get to the hospital after news of his mom being admitted to the ER. Maybe, just maybe, he didn't have negative intention, only positive.

Always assume positive intention unless someone gives you an irrefutable reason to think otherwise. My mom showed positive intention, often much to the surprise of the rest of us. In her mind, no one ever did anything wrong, and everyone was someone who could be her friend. It was up to them to prove they had negative intention for her to not see them as a friend. So, assuming positive intention puts everyone on a level playing field. It puts everyone you meet as a friend, not a stranger. Change your mindset. Change your life.

> **❝ *We either live with intention or exist by default.* ❞**
>
> —**Kristin Armstrong, professional cyclist**

Sadly, however, there may be times when someone within your inner circle fails you and does so intentionally. What then?

If that toxic person is in your environment, you either have to not let their toxicity get to you, or simply remove yourself from the situation. This could include removing that person from your life—no matter how hard it may seem. It may be hard in the short term to let someone go but continuing to allow anyone to steal your positive energy is a longer-term problem. You don't need to deal with that for a minute longer than you are already allowing.

Oftentimes, when those closest to us fail us, we feel hurt, sad, disappointed. Though, it is important to remember that *we are* the owners of our feelings. It's okay to feel these things, but allowing ourselves to wallow in less-than-positive feelings will only cause us to drown in the sea of negativity, ultimately. Then, we are no better than the person who failed us.

I had a toxic person in my circle once, and I can remember him saying to me, "You are so negative all of the time." I always found this interesting because everyone else in my life would compliment me about how positive I was. So, why was it that he thought I was negative? The most important thing to look for and identify is how YOU feel when you are around them. Are you a different person? The reality was that his negativity and toxicity pushed me to be negative and unhappy around him. I didn't like who I was around him, but I didn't know how to let go of him as a person within my inner circle. So, how do you get back to a positive life quickly?

It's best to quickly identify toxic people before they are able to drag you under. Here are common characteristics to look for in negative people.

N arcissist

E nergy-Draining

G reedy

A rgumentative

T rustless

I rresponsible (for their actions)

V indictive

E nvious

If you have anyone in your life that exhibits even a few of these characteristics, try to back away from them as kindly as you can. Protecting yourself and the work you're doing to develop your positivity is vital! I eventually let go of that negative person in my life. It was not easy. It was hard. But in the end, it was worth it.

"*Even five-minute meaningful conversations with other people not only fuel us in the moment but also build up a reserve of social capital so that when hard times strike, we can draw down on that bank account.* **"**

—**Michelle Gielan, American broadcaster**

Chapter 8

Outer Circle

I remember one of my "Friday drive" phone calls shortly after Mom started volunteering at Bryan Hospital. She was so excited about her new volunteer position and said, "Oh Amy! I just love it!"

"What do you love most about it?"

"That I get to smile at everyone that passes by the front desk. You know Amy, you just never know why people are in the hospital, what their circumstances are, or who they are visiting, and why. If my smile and simple 'Hello' can make them feel just a little bit better about being there, then I've done my job."

Wow! How incredible! Oftentimes, we feel like we need to do something BIG: volunteer somewhere that is going to change the world and dedicate every bit of our free time toward a good cause. But the reality is, my mom, through her simple act of smiling and greeting others just a few hours per week, did change the world! I strongly believe that when you make an impact on just one person for the better, then that person may pass it on creating a snowball effect that will change our attitudes and change our world.

So, the first time I walked into Bryan hospital and passed that same front desk, where she use to volunteer and greet people, on my way to the ICU to see her after she had been admitted, I pictured her sitting there smiling and greeting me in the sweetest way that only she could do—making me feel okay about the unknown that lay just beyond those hospital elevators.

Kindness of Strangers

"I have always depended on the kindness of strangers," is an unforgettable line from Tennessee Williams's *A Streetcar Named Desire*. Blanche DuBois is a pathetic figure, and the strangers she refers to are less than savory characters. But there is a central truth to her words because the world relies on the compassion of strangers. Whenever a terrible earthquake or hurricane hits, or whenever there is terrible carnage caused by human cruelty, what helps to heal the devastation is the outpouring of generosity from people who, quite possibly, have never visited the country that's been beset by tragedy. That sort of generosity is born of the notion that "we are all one," and it is always heartwarming to see and to participate in.

My mom exemplified this until her last moments. It was always incredible to watch her with the nurses and doctors, thanking them every time they did something for her, even if that something caused her pain. When it was painful, she would respond with an "Owey!" then a "Thank you!" She understood that, even though strangers, generally people are good people, and humanity has good intentions.

What really brings home the power of kindness is when we find ourselves the recipient of it. We return now to the concept of the "noble act" we touched on in the M.O.M.E.N.T. section.

Have you ever been the subject of a random act of kindness? It's a very strange feeling at first. When some stranger buys your meal without your knowledge and disappears without giving you the chance to thank them, the experience stays with you for days. You wander around thinking, "Why me? Did I look like someone in need?" Or, more cynically, "What do they want from me?" There's even a twinge of guilt because you know there were probably several other people in that restaurant who perhaps needed that meal paid for more than you did. But I believe that is the point of a random act of kindness: to make you feel that you now owe the universe something. You cannot pay the stranger back for their kindness, but you can enact your own act of random kindness to repay the cosmic debt. Therefore, one act of kindness will lead to another, then another, then another, ad infinitum. Kindness is infectious.

If you've never tried a random act of kindness, give it a go. I'm sure it's not for everyone, and the temptation to stick around and see the reaction of the beneficiary will be almost too strong to resist, but it is a great exercise. However, if the idea is too way out there for you, or you're too worried about whether the target of your random kindness is deserving enough, then try a version of it with acquaintances, rather than perfect strangers. Coworkers make great targets for acts of kindness. Celebrate their achievements, both professional and personal, and brighten their day in unexpected ways. Or simply buy the entire team a tray of cupcakes, or make sure everyone gets a greeting card on their birthday. Your kindnesses don't have to be extravagant (and in fact this makes people uncomfortable), but they should be heartfelt.

Another way of showing kindness is getting involved in community events or with local organizations that need your help from time to time. Feeling useful and appreciated is key to maintaining your own positivity, so by volunteering, you can serve others AND serve yourself.

"Carry out a random act of kindness,
with no expectation of reward,
safe in the knowledge that one day
someone might do the same for you."

—**Princess Diana**

Community in a Digital Age: Lipstick Therapy

Without a doubt, the way humans connect has changed radically, and the rate of change has unsettled many people (especially those over a certain age). But the digital revolution is nothing to fear; it's simply the latest stage in a long history of human communication evolution. Like any means of communication, the Internet is only as good (or bad) as the person using it.

I, for one, choose to see the digital age as a positive thing. For one thing, there's no going back, so you might as well embrace the good! But more than that, I believe it brings people together who would never have met in a pre-digital era. Sure, it can disrupt our inner circle sometimes—after all, we've all cringed when we've seen families in restaurants when each member of that family is focused on their own devices, not each other— but there are two ways in which the digital age does wonders for our outer circle.

Insights into other people. The internet has made the world more accessible, and it is a window on all sorts of cultures and experiences we would never have otherwise encountered. The world is a wondrous place, and thanks to the internet, there is no place you cannot visit, no person you cannot talk to, if you want. The internet enables us to be global citizens, and the sense of gratification for feeling globally connected can be huge.

Collective empathy. Before the internet, a collective response to tragedy was almost impossible, and certainly more time-consuming and costly. Now, hundreds of thousands of dollars can be raised in a matter of hours online, and people can instantly express their solidarity with their fellow human beings. But, more than its fundraising power, the internet is the most effective way of raising a community—creating a group of people who are supportive of a cause (beyond a one-time donation).

The power of online communities was brought home to me when my mom's diagnosis was given. She had surgery to remove the tumor, but she wasn't waking up. She was in a coma for over a week, and every day we wondered if that day was to be the day she would pass away. The grimness of the situation was overwhelming. One morning, at my parents' house, I got ready to return to the hospital. I opened a cupboard and found my mom's enormous lipstick hoard; the woman must have had forty colors in there! I just thought to myself, "Who the heck needs forty different colors of lipstick?" Then I reached for the brightest color of lipstick I could find—a ridiculously bright pink.

I put on the lipstick and went to the hospital. Before backing out of my parents' driveway that morning, I took a selfie and posted it online with the caption: "If this bright pink lipstick is not going to wake her up then I don't know what will. #lipsticktherapy." And from that, from that single hashtag, an entire community emerged, and other people started to use the hashtag as well. Every time I was at my parents' place, I would put on a different color of lipstick and post a picture and caption on social media using the hashtag lipstick therapy (#lipsticktherapy).

Then one day, feeling very emotional, I realized I wasn't coping with the constant demands from friends and family for updates about my mom's condition. The text messaging was constant. It was either my friends, my brother's friends, or my parents' friends, or my mom's family or my dad's family, and I really didn't know how to keep everyone updated. What I really wanted to do was just spend some time with my mom. Seeing that I was overwhelmed, one of the amazing hospital staff suggested I set up a Facebook group, and she gave me a few other ideas for communicating more broadly, but none seemed quite right.

But that night when I went home, I decided to do what I knew how to do best: design a website and start a blog. That way, whoever wanted to be kept updated could just go to this website and subscribe for automatic updates about my mom. I called that blog PinkLipstickTherapy.com, and that's where it all started. From there, the lipstick community really evolved.

A month or so later, I was looking at who had signed up for updates about my mom and found that we had built a global community of people who were following her story—people we didn't even know. People had started sharing it on their own social accounts, and that's how other people started following it; suddenly, people we didn't even know from all over the world were following her story.

It was very humbling to realize that we were making such a broad impact simply by sharing her story; something that started from a single hashtag on social media. And I believe that the secret of this success is that my mom's story wasn't so much about a woman dying of brain cancer as it was a story of hope, love, positivity, and perseverance in the face of adversity. That's why I think people latched onto this story. Even ten years ago, we never would have been able to have this outcome. That's the positive power of the social media explosion.

Negativity Filter

I know, however, that people do have very negative experiences when they put personal information out there. There are (and always have been) trolls—people who delight in tearing others down, and social media makes it incredibly easy. These people would never say such things to your face; they are simply cowards who hide behind avatars and false identities. They are NEVER worth engaging in dialog, because they are angry, unhappy people who are probably incapable of taking on any of the lessons this book has to offer: sadly, some people are beyond help.

We have the power to filter out these people. But we should also be filtering our negativity. Sometimes, we simply have no clue how toxic we're being online! Think of the people you're connected to on Facebook—most likely people who sit in your outer circle—and I'm willing to bet there are plenty of people whose posts you skip over, knowing their pages are a litany of misery. But have you checked your own page lately? If not, take a moment now to review your last ten posts. How many were upbeat? How many were complaints?

Social media can be cathartic. It offers us a place to vent our frustrations and get some instant feedback from people about our right to be mad, sad, or bad. But is that the kind of image you want to put out about yourself? Is that the kind of vibe you want to give out to the world? There is simply too much negativity in our social media feeds, so make a commitment to stop contributing to it.

In fact, I enjoy the experience of being on social media, but that's a choice. I've made that choice not only for what I post and put out there but also for those people I follow and choose to be on my feed. Any time I see a stream of negative posts, I just unfollow the person or hide their updates because I want to be in control of my life and in control of my social media. I just remove myself from those negative situations.

But then there are the people whose posts are relentlessly positive, so much so that you doubt those people are telling the truth about their lives: how could they possibly be so damn perfect?! These upbeat posts can be just as anger-making as the negative ones—but that's only because you're probably unhappy with your lot in life. Who cares if they're making it up? Who cares if they're boasting? The only way to enjoy these posts is to work on your own happiness, so they don't fill you with jealousy the next time the friend's perfect life pops up in your news feed. When you're happy, you are able to celebrate their life with them and encourage them to keep sharing the good things.

Activity: Social Media Review

Look back through all your social media accounts. Find five recent positive posts and five recent negative posts. Then assess the following:

1. Is there a pattern to your negativity? For example, are your downbeat posts about politics, work, your family?

2. Once you've identified a pattern, think of one way you can mitigate that trigger, i.e., how can you feel better about that source of negativity?

3. Then, look at the responses you got to your negative posts. How do they compare to the "likes" and comments you get for positive ones?

I have a hunch that more people will respond to your positive posts than the negative. If so, this should be enough to encourage you to post more positively. If more of your friends and followers are taking the bait of your negative posts, by posting more positively, you may be helping to raise the positivity levels among your social network.

In a World of Chaos

We live in a world of chaos. I say this statement all the time, and it's true. Hurricanes, earthquakes, war, famine, riots, shootings—the list of craziness and carnage goes on, and it's easy to be disheartened by events that seem so out of our control to prevent or react to.

It sounds very negative. And you might wonder why somebody like me, who's supposed to be living a positive life, would make such a negative statement. I think by defining the word "chaos" upfront, it really helps us position ourselves and do better for the community and the world.

So, in my view, what "chaos" comes down to is this: confusion. What upsets us about "chaos" is that we just don't understand why something so bad could happen. For example, consider the recent Florida Parkland school shooting. Beyond the fact that it's a negative, very sad, traumatic event, people are confused about why somebody would want to take seventeen lives. Or think of Hurricane Irma that tore apart the Virgin Islands, Puerto Rico, and parts of Florida, or the Las Vegas shooting, or 9/11; our sense of confusion is overwhelming and contributes to our sense of chaos. These big events make us feel helpless. We watch them unfold on the news or social media, and there's just nothing we can do. To me, being caught up in events we cannot control is what chaos means.

We've always lived in a world of confusion. Look at history. We have seen this time and time again. It's not just now that the world is in chaos. The twentieth century was filled with conflict—the Great War, World War II, the Vietnam War, Korea, Afghanistan, Iraq. So much carnage, much of it inexplicable and unjustifiable. The twenty-first century is no less crazy so far, with even our weather systems literally turning everything upside down. But the difference in the last decade has been the way we receive information about events. Once upon a time, we accepted what we were told by government propaganda: life was simple. A lot of times, we were shielded from all the stuff that was truly happening. Today, we believe the world is getting worse and that it's more chaotic and more negative than it's ever been, but really it's just that we're exposed to that negativity and that chaos more than ever before.

My mom's brother, Terry, was in the Vietnam War. Every night, my mom and the whole family would wonder whether he made it through that day. The way they would find out whether he had lived another day was by gathering in the living room and watching the news that night as all the names of the fallen were listed. Can you imagine the stress and what that must feel like sitting in front of a television just hoping your brother's name does not show up? What a way to find out!

Terry made it back from the Vietnam War, but that is something that really shaped my mom and really showed her what true life is—how deep life can be, and how traumatic life can be, and how life can be over at any moment. I think that was a big part of why, at the end, she said she was not afraid to die. She wasn't afraid of death. She had seen it and lived it so many times throughout her life. It wasn't just the Vietnam War, but later on in life, that same brother died of pancreatic cancer. Her other brother died of pancreatic cancer. Her grandmother died of pancreatic cancer. She watched her mom die of pancreatic cancer.

By encountering a lot of death, she really understood that life is truly, truly precious. Years later, my dad would tell the story about how they went to Washington D.C. My mom went to the Vietnam War Memorial and was deeply moved by the memorial. One of the things she did was to find the name of one of Terry's friends who didn't make it out of Vietnam and traced his name on a piece of paper. Later, she framed the paper and gave it to her brother as a gift.

Be the Change

The events of September 11, 2001, have had a massive effect on the American psyche. The way it unfolded on our screens in real time was devastating, and it marked a downturn in American optimism. On that day, almost 3,000 lives were lost. But the terrorists also destroyed a kind of innocence that has reverberated for close to two decades.

My parents went to the US Tennis Open that year, and they left New York City just two days before the attack. My dad says they had both stood in Manhattan, overlooking the World Trade Center, and had a conversation about the towers, how tall they were, how beautiful they were, and really nothing more than that, just a simple recognition of their beauty. Then two days later, the towers were dust. My mom had a great love for New York, and the events affected her profoundly. They were lucky not to be caught up in it, but like everyone else across the United States, it led them to question, "What really matters?" At that time, my parents were so far away from their family, and my mom especially felt a void as a result of living in Texas while all her family was in Nebraska. After 9/11, those conversations started to surface: *Why are we in Texas? Why are we so far away from my family?* That had a huge impact, and a big piece of the decision for them to move back to Nebraska was because they wanted to get closer to family, and they wanted to get back to their roots.

When you realize that life is so short, you make different decisions. And when you really understand what living in a world of chaos means, you start to take far fewer things for granted. You begin to figure out what means the most to you and how you can get closer to that. Events may feel out of our control, but whether you feel helpless is your choice.

The good news is that, although it's out of our hands, and although we may feel helpless, we still get to make a choice. We get to make a decision to give back to our community and counteract the bad with some good. There are always things that we *can* do, even if the event is on a world scale. Every day, we can make that choice to do something better for the community. We can make a choice to do something better for this world. When we get to make those decisions, then we can effect change because we're doing something we can actually control. Although we cannot control that second plane hitting the building, we can control our actions and what we decide to do as a community (local, national, or global) moving forward.

It's Not the Money, Honey

Sending money to the Red Cross or another aid agency is always a good (and easy) option, but it's not the only one you have. Think of any great disaster, particularly in your immediate locality, state, or country. You could donate money, sure, but what if you were to create an experience around that? What if you were to go to where the tragedy had taken place? What if you were to visit with the families who lost someone, or even just reach out to them? You don't have to travel, but if you just reach out to them, and have that experience with them, and talk to them, and offer some sort of support, not only is it helping the community and the world, but it's also helping you build your connections.

A case in point? My mom, of course. She wanted to give back to her community when she volunteered at the hospital, but at that time, she couldn't know she would be admitted later to that very hospital when we found out she had brain cancer. The connections she had made at the hospital really came into their own when she became a patient.

As they say: what goes around comes around. The more you give out, the more you will get back in life.

Better connections are just one advantage of giving to your community. From a scientific standpoint, the act of giving releases oxytocin. Oxytocin is shown to reduce stress levels, and when we are less stressed, we can feel more connected to others.

So, my advice would be to give in a multitude of different ways, not just monetarily, because if you can create experiences, that is where you can really make a difference.

Breaking the Bad News Cycle

Empathic people take on the sufferings of others as their own. They can't help it. It's a step beyond simple sympathy, which is a more abstract emotion. Empathy is visceral: you feel it in your heart and your gut. For empathic people, the chaos of the world can be all consuming; each sad story layers on top of the last.

As a highly empathic person myself (a trait my mom lovingly passed on to me), I stopped watching the news about eight years ago. I stopped when I discovered I was not getting to choose the information that came to me in the news. The broadcasters choose. The newspaper editors choose. In a world of chaos, that can get intense and negative pretty quickly. I found myself internalizing all this bad stuff that was happening in the world and being intolerably sad after watching the news. That's just not how I wanted to go to bed at night.

When I made the decision, others told me, "You're going to miss out on something!" But I promise you, in eight years, I've never missed any big events. I've never missed out on something that I may need to know about. In a digital world, I can, for the most part, choose what news comes to me. I can choose what websites I visit. I can choose what topics I want emailed to me. I can choose who I follow and who I don't follow on social media. I get to make that decision. The beautiful thing is that those things I don't need to know about, those things that would otherwise consume my mind, don't have to take up space in my mind, and I can use that hour or half hour every night to work on something positive.

Chapter 9
Commit Yourself

An Open Letter to My Mom

Mom,

Do you remember that day when I asked you, "How do you go on in life once you lose your mom?"

You said to me, "You just do, Amy! You are strong. You will be okay."

Sitting at the foot of your hospital bed that day, both of us in tears, I felt less than strong. I didn't feel like it was going to "be okay." In fact, there was nothing okay about this.

It took me thirty-five years to finally get to the point where I viewed you as my best friend, something you always wanted from our relationship. And now, I wanted another thirty-five years to celebrate that, to make more memories as friends, and not just as mother and daughter.

Somehow, I wanted your answer to erase the inevitable. But that was never going to happen because we both knew the end of your life was just around the corner.

I felt . . . lost. Heartbroken. Weak.

We were nearing the end. The last chapter.

We both knew it was your last chapter in life. And although, we all would love to be able to write that last chapter of our own book, none of us get to do that. We don't get to choose the way we leave this Earth. And once gone, we can't come back to rewrite history.

So, I will write your last chapter for you.

It won't be a chapter of sadness, or pity. Nor will it be one of defeat or destruction.

Instead it will be one of positivity and perseverance. One of strength and happiness. One of commitment. Because that is exactly how you lived your life, and you deserve that to be your last chapter.

I love you,

Amy

P.S. Don't worry, Mom. I promise I will be strong.

Perhaps it's fitting that the last chapters of this book are about commitment and choice. After all, if we want to live a life that is bursting with happiness, isn't that what it really takes? Commitment and choice?

Commitments make us happy. The obvious kind is marriage or a life-partnership: we go through public ceremonies to declare our commitment to each other, we wear rings or other tokens of commitment, and we celebrate anniversaries of having made those vows. But the benefits of commitment go beyond romantic love.

We feel good when we fulfill our promises. We feel good when someone comes through for us on something they said they would do. We trust people who deliver on promises, and the commitment of friends lifts us up. Conversely, broken promises can cut deep, and we remember them for a very, very long time.

I remember when I was a little girl, probably in fourth or fifth grade, I wanted a full-size keyboard. I had started playing the piano at four or five years old, and I learned on a little keyboard that we had at home. At my piano lessons, I would get to play on a full-size piano, and I decided that's what I wanted at home, too. My parents finally gave in and said they would buy me the keyboard—a state of the art instrument that you could plug it into other electronic devices. Now it seems like no big deal, but at the time it was revolutionary. They told me: "We'll get this for you if you're committed to continuing learning and playing."

And I said, "Yeah, of course, of course I will!"

So, they got me the full-size keyboard. It sat in what we called our sitting room in our house, and shortly after, about six months after I got it, I decided I didn't want to play the piano anymore, and I quit. My mom never really got angry, but I remember her telling me that she was just disappointed by my broken promise. And that almost hurts worse when your parents are disappointed in you than if they're just upset with you, because if they're upset with you, then you tend to get over that. But if they're disappointed, it goes so much deeper, and that taught me a lasting lesson about commitment.

We don't want to disappoint ourselves, and we don't want to disappoint other people, so we need to make a commitment to stay focused and to continue growing our lives and growing who we are as people.

A commitment that I made, which I kept, was made to my mom while she was dying in the hospital. I committed to her that I would continue to spread this message of positivity. And I will not disappoint her because I made that commitment to her, to myself, and to you, my readers.

Tips for Making Commitments

Know your limitations. You must do the work on your character to know what kind of commitment you are capable of making. When you make a promise, it's vital that you have the capacity to keep it. If your life is disorganized, your capacity for commitment will be restricted, so if you want to do more for others, make it a priority to clear the space for them. Commitments are not easy! That's the point, so you need to sacrifice something if you are to honor your promise to someone else.

Go public on your commitment. I'm not talking about openly bragging about what a wonderful, generous person you are, but rather I'm suggesting you find a way to tell your connections, friends, or family, "I'm gonna do this," because that leads to an accountability factor. You see it on social media all the time with people who are running marathons. Quite often they are running for a specific cause, although they may not tell you why they chose that cause, you can be sure it's because they made a private commitment to a friend or family member. Find ways to share your goals, even if you don't share details of why. Sometimes the embarrassing prospect of public failure can be enough to hold your feet to the fire!

Turn an abstract commitment into a concrete outcome. My commitment to my mom to share her values of positivity took the form of a book—a tangible product, rather than a vague promise. It's a useful technique because it gives your goal a clear set of actual "deliverables" (like the marathon example given above). In writing this book, I had to plan it out, collect the material, organize my thoughts, put down the words, get them formatted into a book, publish the book, and so on. At the end, I'll have something to show for the commitment. Of course, it won't end there, but the moment the book is published, it will feel like a weight off my shoulders. A commitment is a weight, but one you willingly carry because of love for someone or sheer personal integrity. As the French philosopher Jean-Paul Sartre noted: "Commitment is an act, not a word."

Breaking Commitments

Is it ever okay to break a commitment, such as the one I made to my mom? Have you ever been through that situation yourself and realized that the commitment you made, in good faith, is either unrealistic or damaging you somehow? Is there any way that the commitment could be broken in a good way?

When you feel that it's not right, then you don't continue. The point of making commitments is to make someone else happy and, by extension, make yourself happy. When it seems to be making nobody happy, it could be time to let go. It's like being in a bad relationship. You committed to being in that relationship, but that relationship may be bringing negativity into your life, it may not be bringing you what you need to otherwise be more successful in life. If you know in your heart, deep down, *this is not right*, breaking a commitment is not only inevitable but also the kindest thing to do. If something no longer feels right, then stop. If stopping is going to bring you to a better place or a different commitment that you can honor, it will be better for you in the long run.

Right before my mom got sick, I was working for a women's networking group as an event planner for its annual conference. I was also a regional director for them, helping them start chapters in the southeast part of the United States. I had made that commitment to them, and like all companies, they expected me to fulfill my contract and do those things that I said I would do. As soon as my mom got sick, I knew I was not going to have the time or the ability to be able to execute.

Maybe a week after we found out my mom had terminal brain cancer, I had to quit the job. I don't like that word, "quit," but I had to let them know I could no longer can do what they expected of me. I felt bad for putting them in a less than desirable situation, but on the other hand, I knew they would be in a worse position if I delivered but delivered badly. If

I hadn't walked away from that commitment when I did, it would've been worse for everyone.

When you are not going to meet somebody's expectations, it's just best to be honest about it with all parties: be transparent and have that adult conversation.

Your Commitment

So, I want you to make your commitment RIGHT NOW. Commit to the M.O.M.E.N.T. daily practices. Go to the website (www.thepositivelifeco.com/seven-more-days) and download your worksheet. If you are serious about making a difference in your own character, connections, and community, and you want to finally achieve your lifetime goal, then you will do it immediately. You never know when your time is up. You never know when you will find yourself in a *seven more days situation*. So, do it now before it's too late.

> *"There's a higher form of happiness in commitment. I'm counting on it."*
>
> —Claire Forlani, Actress

Chapter 10

The Choice
Is Yours

"I don't want to go." Those were my mom's last words.

As my dad, my brother, and I all stood around her in her hospice room, we tried to comfort her, telling her it was going to be okay. We didn't know how to respond to her plea for more time. So, we all just cried. Truthfully, I didn't want her to go either, but I knew that this was no way to live.

She would go on to live **seven more days** after those last words before she died on December 10, 2016.

Those seven days were filled with agony. Although she never spoke again, she moaned in pain. She became unresponsive—didn't even eat or drink. Imagine laying on your deathbed unable to communicate, just you and your thoughts of your life and soon to be death.

My mom didn't get to choose how she lived her last seven days. But she did get to choose how she lived her life—and she chose positivity, perseverance and happiness. You can too. She understood that character, connections, and community is always a work in progress. And that you always have a choice in life.

In this mini-chapter, I want to leave you with the fact that you have a choice right now. You get to choose to commit to your life, you get to choose to commit to positivity, you get to choose to commit to happiness, and you can commit right now through the M.O.M.E.N.T. daily practices, through the L.U.C.Y circle, and through positivity, so that you can achieve true happiness in life. Because if you just put this book down and don't make the commitment to change or don't make a commitment to be more positive, then you're going to disappoint yourself and fall short of being truly happy in life.

You get to choose how you will live your next seven days. And if you had only *seven more days* left to live, what would you do?

Go. Do that! Do that now—unapologetically. Imagine the possibilities, make a difference, and crush life . . .

. . . before it's too late!

THE END

A SPECIAL INVITATION FROM AMY (IN CASE YOU MISSED IT)

As I scroll through my Facebook memories, I am reminded that I have been fighting for positivity for years. I see my posts that are more than ten years old about living a positive, happy life—not just for my own benefit but hoping to inspire others to do the same. So, although the story of this book may start at one point in my life, the fight has been happening for much longer. And I am not about to give up on that fight now.

I have known for many years now that life is fleeting and the single most important thing in life is to be happy. My hope is that, through this book and through our efforts in The Positive Life Company, we give you the tools, resources, and inspiration to be happier, to be bursting with positivity so that you can live your best life and achieve anything you want.

To continue our relationship, I would like to personally invite you to join The Positive Life Company communities. It's in these communities where we see lives transformed. These communities are about making a difference. They are about being a part of a movement.

Join our free community on Facebook at http://bit.ly/ PLCComm. Whether you are just starting out in your positivity journey, or you've been at it for a while, you will find that you are right where you need to be in this community. We have many who have been a part of The Positive Life movement since day one. They will be there to support you, to love you, and ensure you do this crazy thing we call life in the best way possible!

Or, find a chapter in your area at http://thepositivelifeco. com/find-a-chapter/. If you don't see one in your area and are interested in starting a chapter for your community, reach out.

Feel free to connect with me on any of the social networks. Send me or The Positive Life Company a direct message or comment anytime. I respond to all messages personally. Let's connect!

BONUS: THE 5 DAY POSITIVITY CHALLENGE

If you are still unsure where to start your journey in living a life that is bursting with happiness, join our 5-Day Positivity Challenge at www.thepositivelifeco.com. It will be sure to catapult you into a world of positivity.

73507677R00111

Made in the USA
Columbia, SC
04 September 2019